SUR~~VEYING~~

THE

LEADERSHIP

LANDSCAPE

ESSENTIAL CHARACTERISTICS
OF LEADERSHIP

BY

REV. DR. SAMUEL B. REEVES, JR.

Senior Pastor, The Historic Providence Baptist Church (1821)
President, Liberia Baptist Missionary & Educational Convention, Inc. (LBMEC, Inc.)
President, Liberia Council of Church (LCC)
Vice President, Inter-religious Council of Liberia
Interim President, Grand Bassa University - Grand Bassa County, Liberia

PREFACE BY
REV. TOKUNBO A. ADELEKAN, PH.D.

Associate Professor of Theology and Ethics, Palmer Theological Seminary
The Seminary of Eastern University, St. Davids, PA
Senior Pastor, RISE Community Church of Dayton, Ohio

ISBN: 9798304727273
Published by

Email: improvedint@gmail.com

TO CONTACT THE AUTHOR

Rev. Dr. Samuel B. Reeves, Jr.
3 Downs Street Clayton
NJ 08312-2159
Email: providencehill2@gmail.com
Phone: USA: 616-617-3546 / Liberia 011-231-886-533-941

The proverbs that appear at the beginning of each chapter of this book are all Liberian wisdom sayings and their simple interpretations gleaned from the oral and written culture of Liberia.

These parables attempt to illustrate a wise moral for guarding the essential leadership characteristics of that chapter.

Thanks to:

Lulu Marshall.
Liberian Parables: Wise Sayings and Their Simple Interpretation (Archway Publishing 1663 Liberty Drive, Bloomington, IN, 1015 www.archwaypublishing.com)

and

William BGK Harris.
Liberia's Cultural Great Treasuries: Celebrating Our Cultural Heritage. Improved Solution.com Queetaco Enterprises LCC Atlanta, Georga 2021.

TABLE OF CONTENTS

HISTORICAL PERSPECTIVE

(An updated version from the previous book Surveying the Leadership Landscape: Indispensable Qualities of Leadership, 2022, p. vii)

Almost two hundred years ago, the Christian Church was present at the creation of the Liberian State. In fact, it was at Providence Baptist Church, over which The Rev. Dr. Samuel B. Reeves, Jr., now presides, that the "cornerstone of the nation" was laid. All twenty-six presidents of Liberia have since been professed Christians, leading a largely Christian citizenry.

The ChurchChurch has been intermittently prophetic, endeavoring to speak truth to power, as did past ecclesiastical luminaries such as Episcopal Bishops Samuel David Ferguson and Bishop George Daniel Brown, the Baptist Rev. Dr. E Toimu A. Reeves, Sr., and Roman Catholic Bishop Michael Kpakala Francis, among a host of others.

It is this prophetic tradition that Pastor Reeves invokes as he speaks to post-civil war Liberia's struggle for national reconciliation and identity. However, given the moral ravages of the war, Pastor Reeves summons in this collection of his sermons key leadership qualities directly from the Bible to guide his flock as they exercise their democratic rights. In essence, the emphasis is on what the Bible has to say about these seven essential characteristics of the leader's concern for the work, the leader's ability to pray for help, the leader's ability to lead other leaders, the leader's ability to motivate followers, the leader's ability to organize the work, the leader's ability to handle opposition and the leader's ability to leave the place of assignment better than they met it. With his gifted mind and in the competent hands of Dr. Reeves, these biblical qualities are manifested as they are clearly explained in the Liberian social context with the prophetic echo of, "Thus says the Lord!" and, "Let the church say Amen?"

D. Elwood Dunn, PhD
Professor of Politics Emeritus, Sewanee
University of the South & Author of a two-volume
"History of the Episcopal Church of Liberia."

THE ESSENCE OF LEADERSHIP

By:

His Excellency,
Dr. Joseph N. Boakai
President of the Republic of Liberia

Deacon, Effort Baptist Church
Weaver Street, Paynesville,
Liberia West Africa

A true Leader has the confidence to stand alone;
the courage to make tough decisions;
and the compassion to listen to the needs of others.

He [or She] does not set out to be a leader,
but becomes one by the quality of his [or her] actions,
and the integrity of his [or her] intent. In the end,
leaders are like eagles...

They don't flock.

You find them one at a time.

FOREWORD

What would you say if you were to encapsulate the notion of leadership into a single word or tagline? Influence, vision, results, character, inspiration, and unshakable confidence, organizing people with purpose and empathy, setting a new direction, and navigating unprecedented change.

I have known Dr. Samuel B. Reeves Jr. for over 30 years. He is dedicated to leaders who prioritize God's work, foster praying that relies on divine assistance, and motivate others to live meaningfully. Dr. Reeves has created a legacy of betterment for others to emulate through the many important roles he has held locally and internationally. His specialty is marrying tasks with talents and resolving conflicts with love.

In writing another book that adheres to biblical teachings, Dr. Reeves has crafted a succinct, reader-friendly, and practical framework. He aligns critical decision-making with ethical principles. He insisted that high productivity and performance standards are baseless and dangerous without appealing to virtuous thinking and righteous values.

The chapters are arranged implicitly around spiritual characteristics, challenges faced, and the network of actions necessary to overcome obstacles and solve pressing problems. This approach is compelling. How so? It permits the book to connect with leaders committed to admirable achievements, taking risks, and rallying followers around visionary strategies. It also focuses on uncompromising Christian convictions, which produce mutual trust, justice, genuine service for others, and honesty.

The book aims to highlight the need for morality in leadership. The African folkloric tradition "When the sky is empty, so are the rivers" still sparkles with relevance. Suppose leaders are not governed by divine principles of discerning the difference between right and wrong and being sound stewards of their spiritual gifts and talents. In that case, they will inflict untold pain on followers and manufacture social chaos and economic calamity in their communities. Sam's knowledge is truly broad-ranging and real.

He frames his many articles, lectures, sermons, and leadership experiences within the current events being experienced by the good people of Liberia, West Africa. Yet, his endearing message is a root-belief summary of deeper claims behind and beneath the tumultuous circumstances that inform how leaders should think and behave as they interpret the world around them.

My parents used to say to me, "Son, no matter how high eagles fly or how many flocks of birds sail through the heavens, the sky is never afraid of them." Pastor Reeves is fearless in his cry against all forms of injustice. His quest for truth, love, forgiveness, hope, peace, second chances, and human flourishing cannot be ignored. His mission to make the wounded whole is essentially theological. Therefore, his ideas do not recoil from the threat of political isolation, creeping violence, or the notion of losing personal freedoms.

Rev. Dr. Reeves thirsts for each of us to identify with divine faith powered by grace. Once we embody the message of this book, we will learn to balance accountability to God with nurturing the best potential in others. This is how leaders add value to every word and action.

Dr. Isaac Newton
Trained theologian, educator, leadership consultant, and development specialist.
Coauthor of the book Steps to Good Governance
President of Paramount Communication & Marketing, LLC.

PREFACE

The Call to Commit

Have you ever witnessed a declining organization or decaying community teetering on the brink of death? Then, a new leader arrived, and everything changed dramatically for the better. Anxiety left the building. Trust moved to center stage. Empathy and humility took their respective positions. Petty differences disappeared. Folk began to "lean" in. Sharing was no longer a scarce commodity. The comeback was underway. Alas, I hope the unborn begins to breathe again. The corporate body language changed. Optimism was in the air everywhere! This is the signature of wholesome leadership.

Perhaps you have been part of such an experience, a movement, a turn-around. You may have had little hope for the survival of the organization, community, or nation. Then came "walking in grace," a leader who inspired people to summon their best selves, and you were astounded by the difference. Was the present cast of characters operating under the same conditions and facing the same limitations? The difference has nothing to do with their circumstance or conditions.

It has everything to do with leadership. So, who does the God's leader serve? In a certain sense, it's an easy question to answer: the servant-leader serves God and neighbor. But then the follow-up question is, How? It is this two-pronged question that Dr. Samuel Reeves has addressed in his scholarly vision.

The Rev. Dr. Samuel B. Reeves Jr.—the Senior Pastor of the Historical Providence Baptist Church, the current President of the Liberia Baptist Missionary and Educational Convention, Inc (LBMEC), and President of The Liberia Council of Churches, has written a book that is instructive for anyone, everywhere, with leadership potential and leadership aspirations. This book serves not only those who have a conventional leadership profile but also those ordinary people who are invested in bringing critical improvements to their own context (family, organization, community, or even nation)—but who are not exactly sure what qualities are necessary to make a meaningful, lasting impact. The salient virtues that Dr. Reeves brings into relief are portable, translatable, and de-localizable. In sports, folks would say that these virtues "travel." They perform both at home and away. In sum, these moral dispositions and habits work in all contexts.

The Commitment to the Calling

Perhaps what allows Dr. Reeves to write such a substantive treatise is his heroic capacity to navigate what theologian David Tracy has called the three primary "publics" that govern modern civil society. Dr.

Reeves, like notable world figures Nehemiah (Jerusalem), John Calvin (Geneva), Martin Luther King Jr (The United States), and Bishop Desmond Tutu (South Africa), has brought "sweetness and light" to all three publics. He is a citizen, an intellectual, and a believer. Any specific theologian or minister may, of course, find her or himself focusing more on the conversation with one public over another at various times and in different contexts. More broadly, however, the theologian serves the public of the wider society, the academy, and the Church; through this, the theologian—in this case, Dr. Reeves as "shepherd," "scholar, and "statesman" serves both God and neighbor.

Central to Dr. Reeves' membership in all three publics is his indefatigable zeal to bring wisdom to bear in these interdependent spaces in a manner that raises the moral, social, intellectual, and economic capital of the society (and the human social economy), as an organic force. The wider society, the academy, and the Church are voluntary associations and theatres of profoundly meaningful ethical engagement and substantive social change. What burns through these pages are Dr. Reeves' deep feelings of gratitude for and responsibility to each of these three publics. This is the rarefied space that Reeves occupies. His single-mindedness as a thought leader and public servant has allowed him to excel as a visionary steward of these affairs in Africa and North America. Hence, Dr. Reeves is uniquely qualified to produce a work that illuminates the ethical dimensions of the historical personage, Nehemiah, as a model for personal transformation and then, in turn, helps us to deploy his leadership "arts" as resources for social rehabilitation and global regeneration. Indeed, it is a towering achievement. This is so because Dr. Reeves is deeply concerned with the psychological and cultural effects of power on those individuals who wield it as well; he harbors a deep sensitivity to the terrors and sufferings of ordinary people.

These pages burn with Dr. Reeves' deep sensitivities as a global servant who serves God and neighbor. He does so through a commitment to participating in public conversation about how to realize a subject of genuine individuality, equality, and morality. Like President Nelson Mandela and President Barack Obama, Dr. Reeves intends to make the nation-state a viable site for healing the world's hemorrhaging. He spells out in concrete terms the questions that all people, in some way or another, ask in their everyday lives.

The Characteristic of the Calling

He is a prayer warrior, public servant, courageous visionary, sacrificial strategist, national mobilizer, civic peacemaker, champion of national reconstruction, decorated statesman, and a serial overcomer. The life of Nehemiah is a model for servant leaders who are invested in ego sacrifice and the interest of community revitalization. So yes, this book has a primary target, but it is also reaching for some collateral impact. The genesis of the object lies in the desire to communicate to a nation a vision of what authentic, integral, servant leadership looks like, emphasizing how personal learning and spiritual growth are connected, social cooperation and nation building, and how, together, these constitute practices of ego sacrifice, and spiritual growth, social regeneration, and historical betterment.

Instead of focusing on how leaders think—distilling moral leadership into an intellectual formula—this book focuses on what authentic leaders do to serve with authenticity, dignity, and humility—articulating the shaping of successful moral statesmanship as it is embedded in the practices of biblical formation. In short, for Dr. Reeves, the goal of this practical guide is to push down through abstract theory and sheer fideism, to develop a useful, teachable leadership guide, and to consider what that means for the task of social reconstruction and national rehabilitation.

Dr. Reeves' potent work brings into stark view the hidden gem of leadership; it is not your own noteworthy, public achievements that inspire and encourage those around you to run the race with excellence and courage; it is the practical moment-to-moment, daily, oftentimes peculiar choice as the servant leaders that God uses for spiritual growth and ministry maturity. Great leaders sacrifice self-significance, self-importance, and self-promotion to live incarnationally and increase productivity, regardless of the challenges, conflict, or controversy. Dr King once quipped that the test of a man is not in times of comfort and convenience but in times of conflict and controversy. God uses consistent leaning into this "art" to transform our ordinariness into his living stones.

Calming the Crisis

From Monrovia to Manhattan, Midtown, Lagos to Los Angeles, and London, we live in an age of intense political tumult and cultural upheaval. It appears that one world is dying, and many worlds are powerless to be born, to borrow loosely from Matthew Arnold, the prolific British cultural critic. We seem to breathe the toxic fumes of anxiety and pain. Distrust, division, and depression vie to form a lethal cocktail. Adding to the mix of social and political problems is the decline of church attendance, the growing suspicion towards once credible social institutions, a disregard for the rule of law, a flight from an authority, and a deepening disgust with religious and political leaders on all levels of society. 'Mud and blood' seem to be the order of the day. Guns and bombs have always been big, but today, they seem the only business. If there are doubts that our problems are not acute, the recent conflicts in Europe, Africa, and the Middle East should signal loudly and clearly that all is not well with our global house. We seem to be intent on burning our home to ashes rather than sustaining a living and thriving cosmos. There is an underlying anxiety set to explode at every turn.

Fortunately for us, Dr. Reeves is the drum major for a widening chorus of global stewards who understand the fragilities and frustrations of the age. More leaders like Dr. Reeves are responding to God's call to search for biblical answers that will help hurting people and decaying communities. Reeves meets this need by integrating the truth of God's word with leadership, inspiration, and formation tools. He has sought to develop a biblical worldview, to demonstrate the relevance of the gospels, and to set biblical principles and best practices to the field of social reconstruction. If we are convinced that Jesus Christ is the answer and that the truth of God's word sets people free, then such core beliefs must be integrated into the practice of any viable Christian-informed program of social redemption.

Surveying the Leadership Landscape wrestles with the words and actions of a singular human being who rose to the summit of international geopolitics; it also measures the moral and soil currents that his life captures and conveys and offers leaders an informed analysis that leads to best practices. Although Nehemiah, the builder, was prepared to face the task of organizing degraded and downtrodden people, he found himself facing vitriol and opposition of an uncommon sort. You, too, may feel that you are leading in a dysfunctional environment, and you may sense that your training and qualifications hold you back more than they carry you along. If you scale the mountains of ministry and nation-building, you must recognize what tools to pack and what to leave behind. There is no better guide than Dr. Samuel Reeves.

Finally, reading a book is never enough to change a person, community, or nation. What has the potential to make one better is their response and application. I would not advise that one take shortcuts with this book. If you are an emerging leader, I recommend that you spend seven weeks, about fifty days, on this book, working your way through the book—one week for every chapter. Read the chapter and follow each habit closely. If you allow each chapter to sink in and flesh it out before going on to the next one, I believe that, in time, you will reap the positive changes that will occur in your leadership. This book is a must-read.

Unlike many authors, Reeves has shown in the confessional-religious space and public square that these tools work. They represent more than the insights of professional development. They highlight his calling, his vocation!!! For Reeves, leadership is a process, and anything you can do to amplify what you are learning helps you to make it more permanent. Reeves is a living exemplar, and God is a reward for those who faithfully need him. Take time with it. Read it. Sit with it. Digest it. Apply it!! Triumph!! The Harvest is White!!! In the spirit of Nehemiah, you will do great work and won't come down!! (Nehemiah 6:3).

Tokunbo A. Adelekan, Ph.D.
Associate Professor of Theology and Ethics
Palmer Theological Seminary
The Seminary of Eastern University
St. Davids, PA
Senior Pastor
RISE Community Church of Dayton
Dayton, Ohio

ACKNOWLEDGMENTS

This book, Surveying the Leadership Landscape: Essential Characteristics of Leadership, is the sequel to Surveying the Leadership Landscape: Indispensable Qualities of Leadership. Like the first book, this project was also the passionate effort of a community. Just like it takes a village to raise a child, it also takes a community of caring and focused individuals committed to ensuring the finished product is worth reading.

It is my pleasing duty and praiseworthy responsibility to show my sincere gratitude, deepest appreciation, and acknowledgment to the many contributors and helpers who made this project a success.

Thanks to all of you who spiritually, physically, emotionally, morally, and financially contributed in one way or another to make this community effort a success story. Thanks for your wisdom, constructive criticism, theological challenge, and inspiration to translate this into everyday practical application in these critical times. This journey was successful because you walked with us, held our hands, and whispered sweet words of encouragement. In this spirit of heart-felt gratitude, again I say in the Liberian way, "Thank you OOOOOOO, thank you yah."

To the community of volunteers and staff (Rev. Christopher W. Toe, Executive Secretary, Bishop Samuel Quire, First Vice President, Moderator Aboseh Sangee Septer, Second Vice President and Bro. Emmanuel Howe, Treasurer) at the Liberia Council of Churches; the senior staff, and executives of the Liberia Baptist Missionary and Educational Convention, Inc. Rev. Moris Siah, Executive Secretary, Rev. Alphonso Jet Duncan, National Vice President, Sis. Ophelia Hoff, Treasurer, Dea. Ophelia A. Taylor, Finance Chair, Deacon Martin Allen, Recording Secretary, and Bro. George Sannah, Office Assistant, the Liberia Baptist Missionary and Educational Convention, and the historic Providence Baptist Church (1821); the officers and members of Providence, the staff at Providence: Rev. Joseph J. Roberts, Associate Pastor, Rev. Charlotte P. Kaicora, Director of Women and Children, and Administrative Assistant to the Pastor, Rev. Charles O.D. Diggs, Director of Administration; Rev. Aaron S. Lloyd, Youth Pastor; Rev. Clement Woods, Director of Evangelism and Missions; Rev. Atty Maria S.P. Smith, Director of Christian Education; Rev. Laura C. Pritchard, Director of Sister Church Relations; Sis. Rebecca Parker, Director of Property Management; the junior staff; the Deacons; the army of volunteers; the Trustees, Finance and Strategic Planners Executive Director; and the Staff of the Providence Foundation, for their encouragement, support, and love. This book is dedicated to the people of Liberia and God everywhere who are searching for competent leaders to lead them, leaders whose lives and essential characteristics, like the ones dealt with in this book, motivate people to follow.

To Rev. Dr. Isaac James Newton, Rev. Dr. Darrell L. Armstrong, Pastor Paul Anderson, Pastor Galison, M. George, Dr. Bruce Grady, Rev. Derrick Jones, Rev. Mardea R. Fully, Rev. Meredes Delgado, Dr. Marsha Scipio; my brothers, and sisters from another mother. Thank you for your partnership, love, spiritual, moral, and intellectual grace you have showered upon me over these many years of friendship and kinship. To my good friend, big brother, and elder Hon., Dr. Elwood Dunn, my sincere gratitude for your wisdom, encouragement, and support.

To Dr. Joan Collins-Ricketts, an editor extraordinaire with razor-sharp sight and an acute sense of grammar and spelling, I say a big thank you and appreciate your editorial skills. To a group of young and promising scholars, preachers, and future leaders of progressive and community-transforming congregations of the Baptist Convention in Liberia, Rev. V. Larry Reeves, Rev. Joycie Hukpati, Rev. Ben Fahn, Rev. Floyd Foiryolo, Rev. Meshack Gargard, Rev. S. Perrick A. Stephens, Rev. Mark Jackson, Rev. McDonald Saah, Rev. Robert Jally, I extend my deepest appreciation. The future is yours. I am also grateful to sister Hawa Goll Kotchi for adding her editing skills as well.

To my darling Alice in the place, Mrs. Alice C. Reeves, my son, Alfield Cephas Reeves, and all my siblings—Othello, Amanda, Ella, Joseph (Joe Boy), Larry, Robert, Samuel the III, Serena, Henry, and James (looking down from heaven); thanks for your unflinching love, encouragement, help, support, and fervent and ceaseless prayers.

A hearty thank you to the publishing house Improved Publishing Consultancy for making this exciting process full of tedium and the joy of a completed task a reality. All Scripture passages are taken from the New International Version unless otherwise noted.

To the many who have significantly helped put this book together, a BIG THANK YOU!

In His Dust!

Rev. Dr. Samuel B. Reeves, Jr.
Senior Pastor,
The Historic Providence Baptist Church Broad, Center & Ashmun Streets, Monrovia, Liberia
President,
Liberia Baptist Missionary & Educational Convention, Inc.
Congo Town, Liberia
President,
Liberia Council of Churches (LCC)
15th Street, Liberia, West Africa
Interim President,
Grand Bassa University
Paynesberry, Grand Bassa County – Liberia

LEADING
SELF

CHAPTER 1

THE FIRST ESSENTIAL CHARACTERISTIC OF LEADERSHIP: THE LEADER'S CONCERN FOR THE WORK

Liberian Proverbs
"PUT WHIP TO YOUR HORSE."
Move quickly and do what you have to do.
"IF YOU LISTEN TO THE NOISE IN THE MARKET,
YOU WON'T BUY FISH."
Don't worry about what people think; do the right thing.

Introduction

What does it take to truly build a flourishing nation, where the least and the unlovable, the locked out, the let alone, and the lonely can thrive effectively and survive successfully? Think deeply and honestly about your answers. Are you with me? Listen!

This chapter begins a series of sermons on leadership. This series is an election special in honor of Liberia's October 10 Presidential and Legislative elections. Like the 2005 elections, many of you are asking who to vote for, and some of you seem to be sure who you will vote for; several of you have asked me to tell you for whom to vote.

I appreciate the honor, but our job, and my job, is not to tell you who to vote for or for whom not to vote. My spiritual responsibility to you and this Nation is to help you make your own informed, God-honoring, country-loving, Liberia-first-focused decision. A decision that I believe should not be based on your tribal, ethnicity, social connectivity, family heritage, political affiliation, party connection, or even affinity for a particular candidate in the race.

We hope that messages from this sermon series will inspire and inform you to decide who to vote for based on the biblical mandate proffered by the word of God and shared with us by the Prophet Nehemiah, based on the qualifications that show themselves in that candidate's character.

This series begins helping Liberians, individually and as communities throughout this Nation, choose the right presidential and legislative leaders in the upcoming general elections.

Every believer is a minister or servant of God who should serve God and exert influence on others where God has called them to lead. Leadership is one person influencing another person positively. Christian leadership is one believer spiritually impacting others for God's glory.

4

The book of Nehemiah is a practical example of a biblical model of leadership. Charles R. Swindoll calls it a "practical book about leadership."[1] Cyril J. Barber further agreed and argued that a "study of the book (Nehemiah) will enlarge upon three important topics: the basic characteristics of dynamic leadership, the importance of spiritual principles, and the necessity of sound administrative policies."[2]

In 1 Kings (11:11), Under King Solomon, the Nation of Israel was divided. The Northern Tribes were taken captive in 722 BC by Assyria. In 2 Chronicles (36:19), the Southern Tribes were taken captive in 606, 507, and 586 BC. God used three different leaders to restore His people to the land and Himself: Zerubbabel the Builder in Ezra 1-6. Ezra, the Teacher in Ezra 7-10, and Nehemiah, the Layman and Volunteer in Nehemiah 1-13. These three leaders were very different. God knew which leadership styles and unique gifts and talents His people needed in their leaders at various stages of the Nation. For the condition of this Nation, we will focus on the leadership of Nehemiah.

In 2005, after about 25 years of war and destruction, God sent the people of Liberia a leader, President Ellen Johnson Sirleaf.[3] who

---

[1] Charles R. Swindoll. Hand Me Another Brick: Timeless Lessons on Leadership. Thomas Nelson, xi, 1998

[2] Nehemiah and the Dynamics of Effective Leadership, page 14.

[3] President Ellen Johnson-Sirleaf served as the first female democratically elected President and head of state in Liberia and on the continent of Africa. She was the 2011 Nobel Peace Prize winner. Sirleaf was awarded the Nobel Peace Prize for her non-violent efforts to promote peace and her struggle for women's rights. She served as President of the Republic of Liberia from 2005 to 2016. He created

Restored the Nation to the community of Nations from a partial state and returned peace to the Nation. In 2017, God sent Liberia another leader, President George Mannah Weah,[4] who reexamined and evaluated the genuineness of the status of our respectability as a nation and around the world, and have kept that peace, successfully passing several stress tests.

I believe that for this Nation to move forward, solidify the peace we've earned, take us to the next level of growth and development, and soar past where we used to be, we need a different kind of leadership: a Nehemiah type of leader; one who will re-establish the Nation into its' full capacity and turn the corner into a bright and prosperous future.

In this special election edition Sermon Series, we will examine seven Essential Characteristics of the kind of leaders needed in all

---

peace and economic progress in Liberia and strengthened women's rights. President Sirleaf expanded freedom of speech and became an example for other African and world leaders. Internationally known as Africa's "Iron Lady," Ellen, after serving as President of Liberia, is a leading promoter of peace, justice, and democratic rule.

[4] President George Mannah Weah served as President of the Republic of Liberia from 2017 to 2023. President Weah represented Liberia at the international level, winning 75 caps, scoring 18 goals for his country, and playing at the African Cup of Nations on two occasions. Widely regarded as one of the greatest African players of all time, he was named FIFA World Player of the Year and won the Ballon d'Or, becoming the first and only player to win these awards while representing an African country internationally. In 1989 and 1995, President Weah was also named the African Footballer of the Year, winning the official award twice. In 1996, he was named African Player of the Century. He is known for his acceleration, speed, and dribbling ability, in addition to his goalscoring and finishing; he was described by FIFA as "the precursor of the multifunctional strikers of today." in 2004, Weah was named by the great Pele in the FIFA 100 list of the world's greatest living players

spheres of life to re-establish the Nation to its full capacity. Over the next seven chapters in this book, we will share with you the theme: Surveying the Leadership Landscape: Essential Characteristics of Leadership.

Like Nehemiah, we will examine leadership from the perspective of those who show concern for the work God has assigned them to, pray for help and for the people, have the ability to lead up, motivate the followers, organize the work, properly handle the opposition, and leave the place, the office, and the Nation better than they found it. In chapter one of this series, we will share with you the first Essential Characteristic of leadership put forth by the Prophet Nehemiah (Chapter 1:1-4).

Leaders who are concerned about the work get involved in the solutions (VV. 1-4). For the Nation to move to the next level of growth and development, we need God to send us a leader and leaders throughout the length and breadth of this Nation who are concerned for the work. Leaders concerned about the work get involved in the solution (vv.1-4).

The Nation cannot be transformed to the next level with the ruling position leaders who spend more time playing than working, with leaders who spend more of the Nation's resources on themselves than on the people they are called to lead - Legislators in Liberia are the highest paid parliamentarians in West Africa. In the 2023 National Budget, legislators in Liberia will spend forty-three million on themselves. Fourteen million will be spent on the Senate and twenty-four million on the House of Representatives. The Ministry of State, which is the office of the President, will spend fifteen million.[5] The Opposition only spends her time criticizing, and the No Position only sits on it. backside and does nothing![6] Leaders who are concerned about the work get involved in the solutions.

Nehemiah lived in Susa, the capital city of Persia, the most powerful place in the world at that time. He was not a preacher, priest, or Prophet 1:11. He was "the cupbearer," an important advisory position to kings (Genesis 40:9-15; 41:9-13). This position would have been the equivalent of the "Chief of Staff" to the President of the United States or the Minister of State in the office of the President of Liberia, who is the highest-ranking member of the Executive Office and a senior aide of the President. Nehemiah, the cupbearer, would be considered "The Second-Most Powerful Person in the Executive Branch (in Washington or Monrovia)" due to the nature of the job.

---

[5] A quick review of the Approved 2023 National Budget, p. 2. The national budget outlines how much money the government plans to generate and spend in a fiscal year. According to Section 65(1) of the Amendment and Restatement of the amended PFM Act of 2021, the Government of Liberia, through the Ministry of Finance and Development Planning, estimated an amount of US$782.94 million for the national budget for FY2023, which marks the Second Beginning of a New Fiscal Period (January 1–December 31). The government anticipates overall revenue of US782.94 million this year, with an anticipated US672.94 million coming from domestic sources and US110 million coming from external resources. However, little to no funds were allotted to finance projects in the social sectors (Education and Health), and agriculture received no budget, implying that no large capital projects for these sectors were intended to be implemented in this fiscal year.

Nehemiah wielded the same influence on his superiors and had great spiritual influence, as Joseph did in Egypt and Daniel did in Babylon.

Nehemiah was a layman and a volunteer. He took a 12-year leave of abscnce from his work in Persia without pay and volunteered to help rebuild the walls of Jerusalem. He left this soft bed, constant electricity, and running water in the palace in Susa, the capital of Persia, with the King to sleep on a mat amid mosquitoes and malaria in Jerusalem.

Nehemiah asked his brother, who had just returned from Jerusalem, how his people were doing (1:1-2). The answers revealed that Jerusalem was both unprotected and in reproach to God. Leaders who are concerned about the work make great sacrifices and are concerned, and do something about improving the condition of families, communities, and the Nation.

Nehemiah could not imagine sitting still when he was told that the walls of Jerusalem lay in shambles. He had to act. Complacency ought to head the list of all the things a leader should fear. Nehemiah heard that the walls of the city were down and dirty, and filth was all over the place, a disgrace to the Hebrew people. It also meant that the people were unprotected physically (Deut. 22:8) and spiritually (Isaiah 49:14-21). The people, God's people, had no testimony (Psalm 50:2). The enemies of Jerusalem said, "What kind of leader can't even keep the walls up around His city; can't even pick up the trash; can't even fix the schools; can't even supply medication in the hospitals; or can't even keep the people safe from death and destruction." This news burdened Nehemiah, and he knew something had to be done. He became concerned about the work and took on the rebuilding project.

Are you with me? Listen, church, listen, people of Liberia. It is easy to be critical, and followers identify problems. But, like Nehemiah, we need leaders concerned about the work God assigned them to perform, leaders who ask tough questions, respond to realistic answers, and get involved in the solutions. Leaders are called to solve problems.

Like Nehemiah, leaders concerned about the work prepare well and convey confidence and trust to the people. Listen, church; like Nehemiah, it is not the size of the Nation or the project that determines its acceptance, support, and success. The size of the leader's concern makes all the difference. People of Liberia, any leader with passion and concern for the work God has assigned to them, can take their people just about anywhere.

Listen, church, listen, Liberia, because Nehemiah was concerned about the situation and what it would take to bring change to Jerusalem. He saw the need in Jerusalem. The people's problems became his problems and his burden to bear, not a toy to be played with. He rose up, made the necessary sacrifice, left his comfort zone, captured a vision, put a plan together, and inspired the Nation to join him in a national cause.

Are you with me? *Firstly,* like Nehemiah, the Nation needs leaders who see farther than others see. Leaders should be able to perceive and acknowledge the Nation's problems and picture the solution without leaving the solution to chance. We need visionary leaders. *Secondly,* leaders who see more than others see. Leaders who know that the problems need to be solved understand what it takes to solve the problem and how much self-leadership and self-sacrifice are required before assuming the responsibility for the job. thirdly, leaders see before others see. They need leaders who are not afraid of the danger of the work, nor those in opposition to it; leaders who can see the threat, plan accordingly, and refuse to give in to the enemies' plots.[7] They need leaders who remember and act on 1 John 4:4, which says, "The one who is in you is greater than the one who is in the world. " Leaders who are sure, beyond a shadow of a doubt, that God has spoken to them and made his direction clear to them about the future.

Listen, church! Listen, people of Liberia; listen well! No overt miracle happened in this book. No healing, miraculous signs and wonders, or people being raised from the dead occurred in this book. God simply partnered with a leader who was concerned for the work that God had laid on his heart and assigned him to do, provided answers to his prayers, and granted him favor, strength, and wisdom to make a redemptive difference.

Anybody can drive a car, but not everybody has a sense of direction. Anybody in the ruling position, in the opposition, or the no position can steer the ship - can wear the badge with the titles Captain,

---

[7] John C. Maxwell, The Maxwell Leadership Bible: Lessons in Leadership from the Word of God. p. 575-578.

President, Vice President, Senator, or Representative. Still, it takes a leader to chart the course. One concerned with the work has a sense of direction and a desired destination to bring real change and transformation to the Nation. Nehemiah was not the last to weep over Jerusalem (Mt 23:37). I believe leaders today who do not get involved in the solution to their challenges are like those who follow them and only complain about their poor leadership but never vote to change the situation. They have forfeited their right to complain.

The best gift any leader can give themselves and the people they are called to lead is a healthy, energized, focused, and wholly surrendered self to God and self-assured of God's work. Bill Hybels says there are nine steps to being self-assured: First, you must be sure of God's affirmation of your calling; then, you must do whatever it takes to keep that before you. Secondly, the purpose of your call must be crystal clear. Leaders cannot lead people into a cloudy future. The leader must have a clear sense of direction and purpose of the future for oneself in order to have others follow them. You cannot lead others into a future you are unsure of, which is not clear. Thirdly, your passion as a leader must be kept hot! It is nobody's responsibility but yours to keep it burning, and do not be apologetic about it to anyone. It is your call. Fourthly, continue to develop and grow the gift(s) God has given to you for the task He has assigned you.

I know I have the gift of leadership. So, I do all I can, read all I can, attend leadership conferences, and hang out with more mature, smarter, and experienced leaders to continue challenging and developing my gift. Fifth, the leader's moral authority, seen through character and integrity, must always be submitted to Christ. The leader's character is tied to their leadership. Six, the leader's pride must be subdued. Seven: is the leader overcoming fear? Eight: are internal issues undermining the leader? And Nine, the leader must establish a sustainable pace between life and ministry.[8]

Like Nehemiah, we need leaders today who are concerned enough to pray for help and pray for their people. The second mark of leadership is, "He prays for God's people" (Nehemiah 1:5-11), which we will examine in the next chapter.

---

[8] Bill Hybels, Courageous Leadership. Zondervan. Grand Rapids, Michigan. 2002. pp. 186-197,

CASE STUDIES

PASSION - LEADING SELF

The First Essential Character of Leadership: The Leader's Concern for God's Work.

Read the case study from the scriptures below and answer the study questions that follow.

PRAYER TEXT:

NEHEMIAH 1:1-6

The words of Nehemiah, son of Hakaliah: In the month of Kislev in the twentieth year, while I was in the citadel of Susa

Hanani, one of my brothers, came from Judah with some other men, and I questioned them about the Jewish remnant that had survived the exile and Jerusalem.

They said to me, "Those who survived the exile and are back in the province are in great trouble and disgrace. The wall of Jerusalem is broken down, and its gates have been burned with fire."

When I heard these things, I sat down and wept. For some days, I mourned, fasted, and prayed before the God of heaven.

14

STUDY QUESTIONS FOR MEDITATION, REFLECTION AND ACTION

THEOLOGICAL MOMENT

- What about the layman Nehemiah's character helped him refocus and continue to rely on God during his most difficult decision as a leader?

PREACHING/TEACHING LENS

- Do you have a firm and coherent position on character development and personal virtue for your life and for those that you influence?

PERSONAL REFLECTION

- What aspects of your character do you need to challenge and change?

COMMUNITY OUTLOOK

- What project, program, or an act of kindness can you contribute to in your neighborhood that is an expression of your concern for the work God called you to do where you are?

CHAPTER 2

THE SECOND ESSENTIAL CHARACTERISTIC OF LEADERSHIP: THE LEADER'S ABILITY TO PRAY FOR HELP

Liberian Proverbs
"YOU CAN'T PLANT OKRA AND REAP CASSAVA."
You reap what you sow.
"BIRDS DON'T PRAY FOR FEATHERS; THEY PRAY FOR LONG LIFE."
You can work to get what you want as long as you are alive.
"IF YOU CAN'T HELP, DON'T HURT."
Keep quiet if you have nothing good to say about someone.
"ANY CRY GOOD FOR BURIAL."
Something, no matter how small, is better than nothing.

In this second chapter, as we move closer to the Presidential and Legislative Elections in Liberia on October 10, 2023, it is my fervent prayer and hope that Nehemiah's example of the second essential characteristic of Leadership will help shape the minds of all Liberian, registered voters in and out of the country to focus on the future of Liberia, and a new batch of leaders that are God-fearing, prayerful, and skillful in decision making: Leaders that are equipped and fully prepared to lead at all levels: Leaders that are vision-driven, mission-oriented; leaders that are passionate and concerned about addressing the many challenges facing our Nation; leaders that are concerned with addressing the drug issues, rape issues, mysterious killings, the high level of corruption and vices that continue to stand in the way of peace, development, and progress.

I challenge all Liberians this morning, everywhere and anywhere, to lay aside our party affiliations, family connections, friendships, fraternal associations, and tribal ties and elect new leaders who will focus on peace-building reconciliation and economic and social developments.

I challenge all of us to elect leaders who will perform the task for which they have been elected rather than focusing on the title, positions, and themselves. Liberians, if we must rise from the ashes of violence and rebuild a new Nation with new leaders, we ought to walk circumspectly and be faithful in our dealings with each other. We ought to be exemplary in conducting ourselves irrespective of our political affiliations. We ought to abstain from all forms of violence, remembering that war is not the answer but peace. Indeed, if this Nation must rise up and live out its true meaning and purpose, then we need new leaders with a new vision, a new sense of direction, and higher commitment; leaders who are willing and ready to rally the Nation through Fasting and Praying, and seeking the face of God through praise, adoration, confession, and claiming God's promises.

"Leadership is a high calling. It should not be done purely for personal gain, goal, or accomplishment. It should have a much higher purpose than that".[9] Great Leadership has the potential to motivate, inspire, guide, and teach others to become better. A good leader creates a vision for others to follow with a goal and cause they believe in. Leaders set examples to bring about positive changes in a nation, church, and community.

Why is Leadership so important at this time in our Nation's History? It is because "Everything rises and falls on Leadership. "This means that the success or failure of any endeavor depends on the quality of its Leadership. It also implies that Leadership is about having authority, influencing others, and adding value to their lives.

However, Leadership alone is not enough to achieve the desired outcome as other factors are involved".[10] A nation that prayerful leaders govern, leaders that are constantly standing in the gap/praying for the people, acknowledging the sins of the people past and present, and acknowledging their own sins, that Nation is bound to succeed. Leading a group of people is never easy, but with faith in God and the

---

[9] Ken Blanchard. Leading At A Higher Level. FT Press May 14, 2023.

[10] John Maxwell

use of prayer, all things are possible. In the words of Jesus, "Some things will only come by fasting and praying" (Matthew 17:21 NIV).

If you take a vibrant church, organization, institution, or Nation that is living out its vision and mission because of competent, God-fearing, and prayerful Leadership and place that Nation in the hands of playboys and playgirls, incompetent, unprepared leaders, no sooner will the Nation lose its focus and become an object of ridicule.

On the other hand, take a nation that has become an object of ridicule and place it in the hands of God-fearing, prayerful, and competent leaders, and watch that Nation rise from the ashes of violence and become a nation of paradise.

In chapter one, we were reminded that concerned leaders are farsighted and can see more than the rest of us. In this chapter, we will deal with the second essential characteristic of Leadership: the leader's ability to pray for the people; the leader prays for help.

Growing up in Children's Church in the historic Providence Baptist Church, we learned that prayer is the key. Not only is prayer the key, but prayer is the master's key. Jesus started with prayer, and He ended with prayer. Prayer is the master's key. Prayer is the key that unlocks impossibilities. Prayer can change a leader's difficult situation into a great victory. The old folks say prayer is the "key to heaven, and faith unlocks the door." Prayer can turn dark yesterdays into a bright future of hope and transformation in the life of a leader, church, organization, or Nation.

Leaders may have doubts and fears; their eyes may be filled with tears because of the many challenges they are confronted with; they may lack the wisdom and courage to lead, but they can go to God in prayer. He knows their every care, and just a little talk with Jesus will make things alright. The Hymnologist Joseph Scriven was right when he wrote:

"What a friend we have in Jesus,

All our sins and griefs to bear!

What a privilege to carry

Everything to God in prayer!

O what peace we often forfeit.

O, what needless pains we bear,

All because we do not carry,

Everything to God in prayer."

Nehemiah, a refugee boy, a volunteer, a cupbearer to the Persian king Artaxerxes, a young man in a position of honor, took some time to inquire from his brothers back home. The report he received brought tears to his desolate heart. He was broken and in tears when he learned that the walls of the city of Jerusalem were broken down, meaning that the city was exposed to both external and internal aggression from forces within and without. With the walls, they were safe; they were protected from outside forces. So, Nehemiah decided to rebuild the city walls, but first, he needed to talk with Jesus on behalf of his homeland, Jerusalem, and his people by praying to God. Christian author. Steve Moore once said, "If God has called you to lead a ministry/nation, He has also called you to intercede for that ministry/nation." It is indisputable that prayer is essential to the life of a leader in the face of challenges. This is even more critical when a leader is entrusted with leading a nation and its people.

Nehemiah purposed in his heart to rebuild the broken walls of Jerusalem, but he had to first go to God in prayer on behalf of his people, knowing that they had sinned and fallen short of God's commandments. They had wandered far away from YHWEH. And if he were to succeed in rebuilding the walls of Jerusalem, he had to start with prayer. He had to call on YHWEH, who said in Jeremiah 33:3, "Call to me, and I will answer you and tell you unsearchable things you do not know."

Nehemiah put things in proper perspective. He first sought God by praying for the Nation's sins. He realized that without God, he could do nothing. He understood the power of prayer and what YHWEH can do through prayer, especially when we confess the sins of our forefathers, our sins, and the sins of the Nation.

There is something special when leaders recognize the power and importance of prayer and are willing and ready to look up to the hills from whence cometh all their help and strength. Prayer was so important to our past leaders that they, through a "proclamation, enacted a law in 1883 declaring the Second Friday in April of each year a National Fast and Prayer Day for the prosperity of Liberia, and in grateful appreciation of God's deliverance of the Nation from external aggression". These past leaders understood the vital role of prayer in the life and governance of a nation. They thoroughly understood the importance of prayer and the words of Jesus, as recalled in the Gospel of Mark 9:29. History tells us that in the nineteen hundreds, under the presidency of Charles D.B. King, the seventeen presidents of Liberia and Germany decided to destroy Liberia.

They posted their gunship on Liberian waters, searching for the little Nation. Upon hearing the news, President King, along with his entire cabinet, assembled in the Historic Providence Baptist Church, the birthplace of the Republic of Liberia, Africa's first independent Nation, to seek the face of God against the external aggression of the Germans, who were too powerful for a developing nation.

They fasted and prayed. During their prayer time, the German captain went to sleep and never woke up. Remember church, remember leaders, and remember Liberians, "Some things only come by fasting and praying." Mark 9:29. The leader stood in the gap by praying for the Nation, and God almighty heard their despairing prayers and saved the Nation.

Another instance of the leader praying for the people is when the Ebola virus hit the country, and citizens and foreigners were dying in numbers, with the most troubling news coming from the Centers for Disease Control in the United States that people would die in their thousands weekly. During this unsettling period in our country's History, the Liberian Council of Churches organized a small prayer team under the Leadership of Apostle Dr. Adolphus During. During, the late founder and Senior Pastor of the Soul Cleaning Clinic of Jesus Christ Ministries International, pastor During also fasted and prayed every Friday for God's divine intervention in the Ebola crisis. The place chosen for the national prayer was the Historic Providence Baptist Church, the birthplace of the Republic of Liberia and Africa's first independent Nation, where President King and his cabinet met and prayed when the Nation was under attack from the Germans.

This time, the President of the Nation, Africa's first elected Female President, Ellen Johnson Sirleaf, and some of her cabinet ministers joined in fasting and praying for the Nation. Before our very eyes, we witnessed the power of prayer and the promises of God fulfilled, as found in Psalms, Jeremiah 33:3, and Jeremiah 65:24 (NIV). God heard and answered our prayers and saved our Nation. Liberia recovered first of the three countries affected by the virus even though she recorded the highest number of deaths. Having recovered, she served as a good neighbor by sending some of her citizens to help Guinea and Sierra Leone recover.

I often wonder if our leaders on this special day take the time to fast and pray for the Nation like Nehemiah did, or do they leave it to the church leaders whom they criticize so much? What kind of Nation will we have if our leaders are in the constant habit of standing in the gap facing and seeking the face of God through fasting and praying like Nehemiah did?

God, give us leaders who will always spend time seeking your face, acknowledging the sins of our past leaders, their sins, and the sins of the Nation. Yes, it is good for leaders to be concerned about what God has called them to do, but they must realize that standing in the gap, praying for their sins and the sins of the Nation, opens doors for God to accomplish His plan and purpose for His people.

Leaders ought to stand in the gap for the people at all times. They ought to pray, praising God for who He is and for His Greatness. They ought to pray, confessing their sins and the sins of the Nation. Come go with me as we look at a leader praying for his people who need his Leadership. We find this pattern in Ezra, Nehemiah 9, Daniel in Daniel 9, and Jesus in Luke 11.

Praise for Who God Is (1:5)

Even though the problem in Nehemiah's life was "great" (1:3), Nehemiah focused on his "great" God (1:5). The greater God becomes in our thinking, the smaller our problems become. Prayer is our response to Christ's words, as in St. John 7: "Without me, you can do nothing." Jesus repeated, "Somethings will only come by fasting and praying."

Notice how often "the great and terrible God" appear together in praise to God in the Old Testament (Nehemiah 1:5; 4:14; 9:32; Daniel 9:4). Praise to God puts our problems in perspective.

Nehemiah is an excellent example of a leader who believed and practiced prayer as one of the main ways we influence others. Henry and Richard Balckeby, in the book Spiritual Leadership, argue that there are several reasons why leaders should pray. Most important among them, they say, is that God is all-powerful and can do far more than even the most resourceful leaders. God's promise is open-ended, and they argue, "Ask, and it will be given to you; seek, and you will find; knock; and it will be opened to you" (Matt. 7:7 NIV).[11]

If someone is angry with a leader, reconciliation might look impossible. But God can melt the hardest heart. Leaders can be stymied when people refuse to cooperate. But God can change people's attitudes overnight. There are times when even the most powerful CEOs in the world can do nothing but retreat to the privacy of their executive office, pray, and let God work." Let God move in your situation as a leader. According to Henry and Richard, "When Nancy Reagan was diagnosed with a malignant tumor and had to undergo a mastectomy, her husband, though he was President Ronald Reagan, realized that even being the most powerful executive in the world had its limits. Commenting on that day, Reagan confessed: 'For all the powers of the President of the United States, there were some situations that made me feel helpless and very humble. All I could do was pray, and I did a lot of praying for Nancy during the next few weeks."[12]

---

[11] Henry and Richard Blackaby, Spiritual Leadership, pages 149-150).

[12] Ibid.

Confession of Sin (1:6-7)

The identification of sin in 1:6 is heard in this petition: "We have sinned against you." After worshiping God's greatness and awesomeness, it is easy to see our smallness and sinfulness. The closer we get to God, the bigger our sins become. This was the experience of Isaiah in Isaiah 6:5. After Isaiah saw the exalted holiness of God, all he could do was cry, "Woe is me, for I am undone. I am a man of unclean lips."

The definition of sin is heard in 1:7. Sin is not only breaking God's rules (1 John 3:4) but also offending a holy God who can be grieved. Someone said, "Grief is a love word. You can only grieve someone who loves you." When we sin, we break the heart of our Heavenly Father. David realized this neglected petition of sin when he confessed, "Against thee and only thee have I sinned" (Psalm 51:4). It is refreshing to hear a leader take responsibility for his sin rather than blaming others.

Claiming of God's Promises (1:8-10)

Nehemiah quoted God's promises from Deut. 28:63-67 and 30:1-5 in his prayer in Nehemiah 1:8-9. Nehemiah had to know God's Word in order to claim the promises of God's Word. About George Muller, it was said he read his Bible on his knees. We should read God's Word as leaders, not to become scholars who impress our followers with our Google knowledge, but we should read God's Word to pray with power for our people.

Surrender to be the Answer (1:11)

Our prayers can move the heart of God to move the heart of the king (Proverbs 21:1). But then we must surrender to be the person God uses to move the king (1:11). It has been well said, "It is great to get answers to your prayers. It is even greater to become the answer to your prayer." God had providently moved Nehemiah into a position and relationship with Artaxerxes to be His instrument of change. In Persian art, the official cupbearer is shown to be next to the crown prince in attending to the king. God has strategically placed each of us in places of influence to pray for and be the answers to our prayers to move people onto God's agenda. Who is the Artaxerxes in your life that God has positioned you near so you can move him to God? Is he your boss at work or your neighbor? Are you praying for the opportunity to impact him for God's glory? Let us ask God to use us to be the answer to our prayers as we lead God's people to accomplish great exploits for Him.

When God has work to do, He will never want instruments to deal with. Nehemiah lived at ease and in honor, but he did not forget that he was an Israelite.

Nehemiah's first application was to God so that he might have fuller confidence in his application to the king. Our best plans in prayer are taken from God's promise, the word on which He has caused us to hope. Other means must be used, but the effective fervent prayer of a righteous person avails most. Communion with God will best prepare us for our dealings with the task God has called and equipped us to do.

In closing, as we draw closer to these critical Presidential and Legislative Elections, let all of us spend quality time first praising God for who He is and what He has done and continues to do in this Nation; let us praise Him for His greatness (Psalms 48:1, Psalms 150). We must acknowledge and confess our sins (Psalm 51:3. 1 John 1:9). We must pray for the sins of our founding fathers and mothers, past and present leaders. Prayer is the key; prayer is the master's key. Jesus started with prayer and ended with prayer, which is the master's key.

I challenge all of us Liberians to pray for the peace and safety of these elections, for our beloved Mama Liberia, just as the disciples prayed in Acts 1: 23 - 26:

> [23] So they nominated two men: Joseph called Barsabbas (also known as Justus) and Matthias.
> [24.] Then they prayed, Lord, you know everyone's heart. Show us which of these two you have chosen
> [25.] to take over this apostolic ministry, which Judas left to go where he belongs."
> [26.] Then they cast lots, and the lot fell to Matthias; so, he was added to the eleven apostles.

CASE STUDIES

LEADING SELF

The Second Essential Character of Leadership: The Leader's Ability to Pray for Help.

Read the Bible case study below and answer the following study questions.

PRAYER TEXT:

NEHEMIAH 1:5-11

5. Then I said: " *Lord, the God of heaven*, the great and awesome God, who keeps his covenant of love with those who love him and keep his commandments,

6. let your ear be attentive and your eyes open to hear the prayer your servant is praying before you this day and night for your servants, the people of Israel. I confess the sins we Israelites, including myself and my father's house, have committed against you.

7. we have acted very wickedly toward you. We have not obeyed the commands, decrees, and laws you gave your servant Moses.

8. "Remember the instructions you gave your servant Moses, saying "if you are unfaithful, I will scatter you among the nations.

9. but if you turn to me and obey my commands, then even if your exiled people are at the farthest horizon, I will gather them from there and bring them to the place I have chosen as a dwelling for my name.

10. they are your servants and your people, who you redeemed by your great strength and mighty hand.

11. O Lord, let your ear be attentive to the prayer of your servants and to the prayer of your servants who delight in revering your name. give your servant success today by granting him favor in the presence of this man. I was cupbearer to the king.

STUDY QUESTIONS FOR MEDITATION, REFLECTION AND ACTION

THEOLOGICAL MOMENT

- What about help that the leader will have to pray for?
- What if the leader does not pray for help?
- Can a leader survive without help from God?
- How important is God in our Leadership?

PREACHING/TEACHING LENS

- Do you have a strong relationship with God?
- Do you call upon Him for help in your Leadership?
- Are you aware that you cannot make it all by yourself?
- Do you know that God's help is available for your Leadership?

PERSONAL REFLECTION

- What was your strength in your Leadership?
- Do you set time to pray, asking God for direction and wisdom to lead people?
- What part of your Leadership is more challenging and will need improvement?
- What are you willing to sacrifice, or what has kept you from seeking God's help?

COMMUNITY OUTLOOK

- What are some of the programs or plans you have for improving your community through your Leadership?
- Do you have leaders of your community who do not know or look up to God?
- How do you intend to help them?

LEADING UP

CHAPTER 3

THE THIRD ESSENTIAL CHARACTERISTIC OF LEADERSHIP: "THE LEADER'S ABILITY TO LEAD OTHER LEADERS."

Liberian Proverbs
"NEVER BURN THE BRIDGE THAT CROSSES YOU."
Never forget where you're coming from;
you may need to return someday.
"WHEN YOUR HAND IS IN BABOON MOUTH,
TAKE TIME TO PULL IT OUT."
When you're in trouble, be careful how you speak
to those who want to help.
"HEART AIN'T GOT BONE."
People have feelings, so be careful how you treat them.

This series continues to challenge us for the Nation of Liberia to solidify the Peace we've earned and enjoyed over the last 21 years, move forward, and take us to the next level of growth and a new season of development, surpassing where we are, we need a different kind of leadership.

For the Nation to rise to the next level and experience a new season of God's blessing and transformation, the next leaders we elect, and leaders in the next season of our history, must lead differently and exhibit the essential characteristics of leadership being shared with you in this sermon series.

In chapter one, we examined the first essential characteristic: the leader's ability to show concern for the work through self-sacrifice and selfless service.

In chapter two, we examined the second essential characteristic— the Leader's Ability to Pray for Help (for the people), the leader's ability to know where their help comes from and stand in the gap for the Nation. Like Nehemiah, we need leaders who know how to pray for help.

In chapter three, we will consider the third essential characteristic: the leader's ability to influence other leaders and lead up. Examining this characteristic helps us understand the leader's ability to know how to lead and follow at the same time. It is the ability to influence others (who have) and receive what you need to succeed in the work God has called you to do.

In the book Courageous, author Bill Hybels talked about the 360-degree leader. The leader with the ability to lead in all directions: To lead yourself - to be sure of who you are and know for sure that God has called you to be, and to do what you are doing; To lead down - to lead people you have influence over; To lead laterally - to lead people with whom you have equal influence, and to lead up - to lead people who have greater influence than you[13].

Are you with me? Listen; in this section of the scripture (Nehemiah 2:1-9), Nehemiah demonstrates the ability to lead up and lead people with greater influence and ability than he.

Author Michael Useen argues that leadership has always required more than just a downward movement. He argues leadership must also come from the top, and today's leaders, more than at any other time, must learn to reach up and lead. More upward leadership has become essential. Leaders who lead up are self-starters who take charge even when they have not been given a charge. Instead of asking if a leader can afford to lead up, today's leaders should be concerned about how we can best lead up.[14]

Listen, church. Nehemiah's ability to lead, to influence other leaders around him and above him, and to receive favors from them, as well as his vision and plan to rebuild the walls as he prepared for the journey to Jerusalem, no doubt resulted from his time of connection with God (vv.5-11).

Leading up brings more to the work you are called to do than you have been given, adding greater value to the company, the institution, or the Nation than it would have achieved without it. Abraham Lincoln

---

[13] Bill Hybels, Courageous Leadership. Zondervan, Grand Rapids, MI., p. 181-197.

[14] Michael Useem, Leading Up: How to Lead Your Boss so You Both Win. pp. 7-8

said that leadership appeals to the "better angels of our nature." Likewise, leading up is a call to improve on the best in the leader's nature.[15] Nehemiah could not afford not to lead up. He found himself in a difficult situation. He had learned to lead himself (1:1-4). He had to lead up and learn from his superiors. He was a servant to a foreign king. He needed a leave of absence. He needed protection letters for the journey. He needed building supplies for the construction project. He needed to know how to lead up carefully and tactfully in order to get what he needed. He needed to lead the King that he worked for to see the importance of what God had called him to do. Leaders who know how to lead up also know the importance of when and how.

After four months (v. 1), he first heard about the sorry condition in Jerusalem before he approached the King, even though he was the King's favorite. He waited until it was his time to pour the King's wine and found an opportunity during a banquet to request help from Artaxerxes. The Kings of Persia were famous for their opulent banquets (Esth. 1:1-12; Dan. 5:1-4), and at some, they were accustomed to granting special requests to those in attendance. Nehemiah knew that. At an appropriate moment during this festive occasion, Nehemiah, as cupbearer, poured the King's wine and conducted himself with grief and sorrow. In his previous audience with the King, he had managed to mask his feelings. This time, the King recognized what Nehemiah intended for him to see, and at once,

---

[15] Ibid. p. 9.

he saw that Nehemiah was not physically sick. Still, he must have been depressed and discouraged about the situation in his homeland. When the King noticed Nehemiah's sad countenance, Nehemiah admitted he was afraid. According to author Charles Swindoll, Nehemiah had good reason to be frightened because those who were noticeably sad or melancholic in the presence of the King were usually killed for 'raining on his parade'.[16]

Faith in the future strengthens the position of leaders who dare to lead those with greater influence than them. However, leadership is required at the top, in good times or bad.[17] Therefore, Nehemiah realized that the welfare and restoration of Jerusalem depended on his negotiation skills. He skillfully asked the King for permission to go home to rebuild Jerusalem. When the King asked about the reason for his sadness, Nehemiah proposed a schedule for the trip and requested safe passage and a supply of material for the rebuilding process.

Nehemiah carefully avoids discussing the present political circumstances of Jerusalem. He did not even mention the name of the city. He knew that the King had stopped rebuilding Jerusalem because of the charge that it had been a notoriously rebellious city (Ezra 4:12-23).

The King responded to Nehemiah with an open-ended question: "What do you want (v. 4)?" Realizing that he was at a crucial point in

---

[16] Charles R. Swindoll, Hand Me Another Brick. Work Publishing Nashville, Tennessee, Thomas Nelson. 1978. page 48.

[17] Michael Useen, Leading Up. Crown Business, Crown Publishing Group. New York, New York. 2001. p.8

his negotiations with King Artaxerxes, Nehemiah paused to offer a prayer to the God of heaven (I Sam 1:13). Like Nehemiah, leaders who know how to lead up first learn how to look up realizing that before you please the kings of this world you must first seek the King of Kings. Nehemiah knew how to express himself with tact. In this passage in vv. 5 & 7, Nehemiah respectfully said to his superior, "If it pleases the King." and "If I have found favor in your sight. Please grant me this request." Those two verses are clinics for leaders to learn how to lead up. According to Andrew Carnegie, "If you want to gather honey, don't kick over the beehive".[18]

Nehemiah did not slam his fist down and demand his rights. He was humble and tactful in his approach when it was needed. J. Oswald Sanders defined tact as the "skill in reconciling opposing viewpoints without giving offense and without compromising principle. . . The same thing can be said in a tactful and untactful manner. One shoe salesman said to his client, 'I'm sorry, madam, but your foot is too large for this shoe.' The other salesman said to his client in a similar situation, 'I'm sorry, madam, but this shoe is small for your foot.' Each used almost exactly the same words, but tact and diplomacy caused one to make a slightly different emphasis by a slight difference of phrasing and secured a loyal and satisfied customer."[19]

---

[18] How To Win Friends and Influence People. New York: Simon & Schuster, 1963, page 19.

[19] J. Oswald Sanders (Spiritual Leadership, page 67).

Nehemiah reminded the King of his faithfulness as his trusted wine steward and servant in this approach. He had served the King well with excellence.[20] Serving with excellence is the best way to learn how to lead up. Do the work assigned to you well and to the best of your ability.

Nehemiah did not make the mistake of underestimating the difficulty of his assignment. Because of the challenges of his job, he had to learn how to lead. He had to be tactful and credible, establish good relationships, and gain the respect of other leaders. He knew that he needed the help of others. He knew he had to learn how to influence others who had more than he had for the journey and to build the wall. Others had more resources - human and financial than he; others had more power and prestige than he; others had more influence and incentives than he; others had more wisdom and work than he; others had more knowledge and know-how than he.

In order for Liberia to move forward, solidify the Peace we've earned, and take us to the next level of growth and development surpassing what we have currently achieved, we need leaders like Nehemiah whose tact and political savvy are matched by a profound faith in God. Leaders who realize that ultimately, it is the gracious hand of God that gives success. The Nation needs a different kind of leadership, a Nehemiah kind of leadership that will re-establish the Nation to its full capacity and turn the corner to a brighter and more prosperous future.

---

[20] The New Interpreter's Bible Commentary Vol.??? pp. 55-56.

Church, people of Liberia, listen; for the Nation to rise to the next level of blessings and achievements, Like Nehemiah, we need leaders who are able to lead up and, with faith, are able to LOOK UP, believing that their help first comes from the Lord; Leaders who are able to lead and influence other leaders at the Economic Community of West African States (ECOWAS), at the African Union (AU), at the European Union (EU), at the United Nations (UN), and the hall of power in the United States (US), to get their backing, their resources, their support, their monies, their connections, their wisdom, and their expertise to bring transformation to our Nation.

The Leader's Ability to Lead Up

Like the other leaders around Nehemiah, listen, the leaders around the world today don't have to share with us what they have, they don't have to share with us their taxpayers' money, and we can't demand from others what we need and don't have.

We need a new kind of leadership in this Nation. The kind of leadership that knows how to lead and influence others. Leaders who know how to build genuine relationships. Leaders who know how to build respect and trust with other leaders in other places and other parts of the world get us what we need for the good and growth of the Nation.

Listen, church, listen, Liberia; this Nation will not rise to the next level of growth and development and receive what God has in store in the next season of our greatness until we find leaders and a leader who has the ability to lead up. Like Nehemiah, leaders who know how to lead up know how to look up and seek first the kingdom of God and His righteousness, and everything else shall be added (Matt. 6:33). Leaders who know how to lead up know how to look up and recognize God's hands upon them. Leaders who know how to lead up know how to look up - from where their real help comes from, because it comes from the Lord who made heaven and earth (Psalm 121:1-2). Leaders who know how to lead up know how to look for the prize of the upward call of God in Christ Jesus (Phil 3:14). Leaders who know how to lead up, know how to look up, will not be put to shame, and their enemies will not triumph over them (Ps. 25:1). Leaders who know how to lead up, know how to look up, waiting for our blessed hope, the appearing of the glory of our great God and Savior Jesus Christ (Titus 2:13).

Leaders who know how to lead are faithful followers. Your fellowship must not be seen as a sign of weakness. You must always recognize your place in the chain of command. Like Nehemiah, you will be most importantly blessed by God because of your humble and godly attitude. Your success as a leader who knows how to lead up - with your superior and others with more influence and affluence than you- will not be because of your people skills or your visionary planning but because God's good hand is upon him.

CASE STUDIES

LEADING UP

The Second Essential Character of Leadership: The Leader's Ability to Lead Above.

Read these Bible case studies below and answer the following study questions.

PRAYER TEXT:

NEHEMIAH 3:1-9

[1] In the month of Nisan in the twentieth year of King Artaxerxes, when wine was brought for him, I took the wine and gave it to the King. I had not been sad in his presence before,

[2] so the King asked me, "Why does your face look so sad when you are not ill? This can be nothing but sadness of heart." I was very much afraid,

[3] but I said to the King, "May the King live forever! Why should my face not look sad when the city where my ancestors are buried lies in ruins, and its gates have been destroyed by fire?"

[4] The King said to me, "What is it you want?" Then I prayed to the God of heaven,

⁵and I answered the King, "If it pleases the king and if your servant has found favor in his sight, let him send me to the city in Judah where my ancestors are buried so that I can rebuild it."

⁶Then the King, with the queen sitting beside him, asked me, "How long will your journey take, and when will you get back?" It pleased the King to send me; so, I set a time.

⁷ I also said to him, "If it pleases the King, may I have letters to the governors of Trans-Euphrates, so that they will provide me safe-conduct until I arrive in Judah?

⁸ And may I have a letter to Asaph, keeper of the royal park, so he will give me timber to make beams for the gates of the citadel by the temple and for the city wall and for the residence I will occupy?" And because the gracious hand of my God was on me, the King granted my requests.

⁹ So, I went to the governors of Trans-Euphrates and gave them the King's letters. The King had also sent army officers and cavalry with me.

STUDY QUESTIONS FOR MEDITATION, REFLECTION AND ACTION

THEOLOGICAL MOMENT

- Why did Nehemiah delay answering the King until he asked for God's direction?
- Why should leaders lead from above?
- Are there positive results when a leader leads from above?

PREACHING/TEACHING LENS

- Why should leaders lead from above?
- What are some of the reasons a leader must lead from above?
- What are some of the benefits a leader can experience in leading from above?

PERSONAL REFLECTION

- Are you leading from above?
- What are some of your experiences?
- Can you, as a leader, succeed without leading from above?

COMMUNITY OUTLOOK

- What are your plans to make other leaders within your community better?
- Do leaders in your community know about leading from above?
- How can your life transform your environment?

SECTION THREE

LEADING DOWN

CHAPTER 4

---◦🔭◦---

THE FOURTH ESSENTIAL CHARACTERISTIC OF LEADERSHIP: THE LEADER'S ABILITY TO MOTIVATE OTHERS

Liberian Proverbs
"ONE HAND CAN'T PICK LICE."
Two people can do a better job than one.
"YOU KNOW YOUR FRIENDS WHEN YOU HAVE TROUBLE."
Real friends, stick around when you need them.
"THE WATER WASTE, BUT THE CALABASH AIN'T BREAK"
You lost what you had, but you can start again.

In order for the Nation to rise to the next level and experience a new season of God's blessing and transformation, the next leaders we elect, and leaders in the next season of our Nation's history, must lead differently and exhibit the essential characteristics of leadership being shared with you in this sermon series.

We need 360-degree leaders— leaders with the ability to lead in all directions: to lead yourself—to be sure of who you are and know for sure that God has called you to be and to do what you are doing; to lead up—to lead people who have greater influence, resources, and abilities than you; to lead down—to lead people you have greater influence over, and to lead Laterally—to lead people with whom you have equal influence and abilities.

In chapters one and two, we learned about the Leader's ability to Lead Oneself. In chapter one, we examined the first essential characteristic of leadership: the Leader's ability to show concern for the work through self-sacrifice, selfless service, and self-assured leadership.

In chapter two, we examined the second essential characteristic - The Leader's Ability to Pray for (the People) and for Help. The Leader's ability to know where their help actually comes from: To be able to stand in the gap for the Nation and its' people in critical times. Like Nehemiah, we need leaders who can pray for help.

In chapter three, we examined the Leader's ability to Lead Up. The third essential characteristic of leadership. To influence other leaders with more resources - human and financial than you; more power and prestige than you; others who have more influence and incentives than you; others who had more wisdom and work than you; others who had more knowledge and know-how than you in order to receive their backing, their resources, their support, their monies, their connections, their wisdom, and their expertise to achieve what God has called you to do.

In this chapter, we will examine the fourth essential characteristic of leadership: the Leader's Ability to Motivate Followers (to motivate others). That is the Leader's ability to lead down. To lead, you must motivate and inspire those people over whom you have greater resources and greater influence.

In What Makes a Leader, Daniel Goldman argues that the one trait that all leaders possess is motivation. A leader with the ability to motivate is inspired by a deep-seated desire to accomplish a task far beyond what others expect and what they expect of themselves.[21]

As a Leader motivated by a deeply embedded desire to start and complete the reconstruction project, Nehemiah gets to Jerusalem, assumes command of the responsibility, and starts the vision, plan, and purpose that God had given him with unusual prowess.

As a Nation, Liberia looks forward to a new day, renaissance, and dispensation. We must be in today, now, to hold the next batch of leaders we elect all over this country to new standards of accountability and leadership so that even when our leaders change from one election circle to another, the standard doesn't change but gets better.

I pray and hope that the leaders and people will hold each other accountable to new standards. And that we can break the molds of the

---

[21] Daniel Goldman. What Makes A Leader. HOR's 10 M st Read. On Emotion I Intelligence. Harvard Business Review Press. Boston Massachusetts. 2015. p. 1.

status quo, the Liberian way, and begin a new day. Are you with me? Listen, whether you lead at home, in the neighborhood, in the community, in civil society, in a business, in an institution, in the church, or in the state, you will take to heart the example of Nehemiah and become a 360-degree leader.

In the passage under consideration in this chapter, Nehemiah shows us several marks of a leader who has the ability to lead down - the ability to motivate and inspire followers - those you need to get the job done, to achieve your vision for the work that God has called you to do. The first mark is knowing how to assess the prevailing situation.

Knowing How TO Assess The Situation VV.11-6.

The journey continues. Four months after this intense burden of being called to the kingdom for the purpose of rebuilding Jerusalem, after he presented that burden and purpose that convinced King Artaxerxes and others with greater influence, Nehemiah goes to Jerusalem bearing the letters that the king issued him.

In Nehemiah's assessment of Jerusalem, what he did was not as interesting as what he did not do. There was no grand celebration or triumphal entry, public announcements, royal delegation, or inaugural ball to celebrate his coming to Jerusalem. In fact, in three days, he didn't do anything, or at least not anything public. Privately, I believe that Nehemiah took a few trusted men to view the walls and the ruin for himself to assess the places, the practices, the pronouncements, the possibilities, the plans, the problems, and the people. Remember, his work had been stopped thirteen years earlier, and the people were pessimistic, tired, and discouraged. With that in mind, Nehemiah didn't tell anyone about the vision that God had entrusted him with. He just li tend, talked, and tried to figure out who the key people in this project would be.

He began to formulate conceivable, achievable, and inspiring plans based on the condition of the walls, the condition of the people, and the resources he had available. In February 2005, I returned to Liberia from Grand Rapids, Michigan, USA, to take up the pastorate at Providence Baptist Church. During the first six months of my pastorate, I did nothing. I observed the church's physical, social, administrative, leadership, and spiritual structure. That period of observation and examination informed how I assessed the situation I met at the church. After the assessment period, I introduced several changes in time management, administration, organizational structures, and leadership management.

The assessment period helped me fully understand where the congregation was and what was happening in the neighborhood, the larger community, and the Nation. It also gave me a clearer picture of what was happening in the congregation. And who were the influencers making things happen at church? The process of transforming this historic congregation from a Deacon-led church into a purpose-driven, staff-run, and pastor-led congregation owes its success to the period of the collective assessment conducted during those early months at Providence. During this period, we were laying the foundation for a new knowledge of leadership that put the needs of the members and the congregation before leadership.

In order for the Nation to move forward and improve, we need a new way to lead, a new kind of leadership, the kind that knows how to discern and assess the status of the problem, the goals, the places, the practices, the possibilities, the plans, and the people around you and ask whether they are discouraged, poised, prepared, apathetic, committed, compassionate, spiritual, corrupt, and compromised.

Like Nehemiah, going forward, the Nation needs a new kind of leadership that will make it a habit to assess and know what's going on. Are the people too poor, are the cities too dirty, the economy too bad, and the country too hard? Are the leaders too wasteful with the Nation's resources? The kind of leadership that prays that God will open their spiritual eyes to see the things they pass by daily. The type of leadership that says that God will help them get unused to the darkness of distrust and division, the sin of the status quo, and the complicity of corruption.

This new period we are about to commence as a nation for growth and development should begin with new evaluation and assessment.

The second mark is Knowing How To Inspire The People VV.17-18.

Nehemiah, already known as a leader of excellent timing, decided on the day and time to share with the people of Jerusalem what God had called him to do and convince them to join him in the national cause of rebuilding the walls of Jerusalem.

In order to move the Nation forward, we need leadership with the sense of timing and the know-how to inspire the Nation around a national cause for transformation. In this text, Nehemiah describes several essential things to inspire people around a cause. The next generation of leaders we elect should know how to exercise these. First, Nehemiah appealed to the people's sense of dignity by addressing the problems in the city. Leaders who know how to motivate followers are effective communicators of vision.

Like Nehemiah, the kind of leadership we need going forward is knowing how to connect with the people's hearts before asking them to sacrifice their time, energy, and resources for the good of the Nation. The kind of leadership we need going forward is the kind that knows how to appeal to the people's sense of dignity (what they are worth), identity (who they are), and responsibility (what they can do to help). Nehemiah successfully rebuilt the walls because he won the builders' hearts before winning the builders' hands. When the Leader tends to the people who work for them, they will tend to the work the Leader is called to do. Despite the Leader's passion for the vision and love for action and achievement, most of their effort must be given to the people. Leaders who focus only on achieving their tasks often end up losing the people and not achieving much. However, leaders who tend to the people usually build up and add value to the people and are successful with the business they are called to do.[22]

Second, Nehemiah was open and honest about the worsening condition of Jerusalem, trying to open their eyes to see the bad conditions they were living in and content with. He challenged the people to commit to a different kind of leadership that loved the country more than the love of self. The kind t at builds a team of inspired followers around them with the same trait. When leaders and people love their job for the work itself and what they hope to accomplish, they often feel committed to the organization that makes that work possible. Listen, church, listen, Liberia, everything is not rosy, and we are not in the best time of our Nation's history since 1847. Don't believe that fairy tale. But all is not lost either.

Finally, Nehemiah assured the people that God's hand was in it. If all of us, including those we elect on Oct. 10, begin to lead differently, things can and will soon change. If you and I believe and pray together that God will open our blinded eyes, we might see God's grace upon us and the hands of all of us involved in the change that is coming to the Nation.

Knowing How To Prepare for Opposition vv. 10,19-20.

In chapters five and six of the book of Nehemiah, we will focus primarily on dealing with the Opposition. However, as a great leader,

---

[22]John Maxwell. The 360 Degree Leader Workbook. Thomas Nel on, Nashville, Tennessee. 2006. pp. 06-20.

Nehemiah prepared himself and the people he had inspired to follow him for the coming adversity, obstacles, and Opposition.

Let's go back and briefly consider v. 10:

When Sanballat, Horonite, and Tobiah, the Ammonite official, heard about this, they were very disturbed that someone had come to promote the welfare of the Israelites.

There are always some people who don't want anything good for others. Listen, like the officials in Jerusalem, there are those today who are disturbed and unhappy that we are talking about leading this Nation forward in new, better, and unusual ways. Why? A new kind of leadership requires a new type of accountability.

Listen to vv. 19, 20:

[19] But when Sanballat, Horonite, Tobiah, the Ammonite official, and Geshem, the Arab, heard about it, they mocked and ridiculed us. "What is his you are doing?" they asked. "Are you belling against the kind?"

[20] I answered them by saying, "The God of heaven will give us success. We, his servants, will start rebuilding, but you have not shared in Jerusalem or any claim or historical right to it."

The two men mentioned in v. 10 and now in v. 19 (Sanballot and Tobiah) were threatened by Nehemiah's arrival. They had an interest in keeping Jerusalem in ruins and didn't know what God had done for Nehemiah. There are folks out there who can't succeed when we do well. Some folks only succeed and prosper when there is ruin and things are not going well. When things are going well, they have nothing to offer. There are Sanballats and Tobiahs in the land. Listen, church, listen, Liberia; there are those out there who are threatened by the change on the way.

Are you with me, church? Listen to every Sanballot and Tobiah in your personal condition or in the national situation. Nehemiah tells us there are two significant ways to deal with your Opposition.

First, to have a God-centered response. To stand on the promises of God. That is, your faith in God's promises to you must guard you in the process of dealing with Opposition. In verse 20, Nehemiah insisted that the God of heaven, the God with worldwide sovereignty (He's got the whole world in his hands), and the God to whom he had prayed way back in Susa? Shushan (1 5; 2:4) would give his success in the wall-building project, and then he reminded the Opposition of his and his associate's relationship with God. Through my spiritually reconstructed imagination, I believe they sang this song:

> We serve a very big God oh;
>
> He is always by our side,
>
> A very big God, oh by my side by my side.
>
> You are God; you are not just big oh,
>
> you are not just God, oh, you are a great God.

That said, it was more than enough to the Opposition about his relationship with this God.

Secondly, Nehemiah maintained a servant's heart and focused on the work that God had called him to do. He reminded those in Opposition that it wasn't his business but God's business he was about.

Are you with me? Listen, Going forward into the new dispensation, our leaders must be reminded that God resists the proud, and if they want His hand to be upon them, they must work toward a servant mentality of humility.

The best thing we can do for those we are called to lead, on a team, in a class, in ministry, in an organization, in a church, or the Nation, is to keep them focused on the promises of Christ, to hold their peace and let the Lord fight their battle and the victory shall be ours. As leaders, we must also consistently assure, reassure, and inspire those accountable to us of the ultimate goal we are working towards - fulfilling God's purpose through our calling. We must keep our eyes on the prize of the upward call of God through Jesus Christ because distractions pull us away, vying for our attention and getting us sidetracked.

CASE STUDIES

MOTIVATION

The driving force behind human action fills with energy and enthusiasm to work with a high level of commitment.[23]

LEADING UP

The Second Essential Character of Leadership: The Leader's Ability to Motivate Others

Read the Bible case study below and answer the following study questions.

PRAYER TEXT:

NEHEMIAH 2:10-20

[9] So, I went to the governors of Trans-Euphrates and gave them the king's letters. The king had also sent army officers and cavalry with me.

---

[23] Ibid., pp. 4-6.

[10] When Sanballat the Horonite and Tobiah the Ammonite official heard about this, they were very much disturbed that someone had come to promote the welfare of the Israelites.

[11] I went to Jerusalem, and after staying there for three days

[12] I set out during the night with a few others. I had not told anyone what my God had put in my heart to do for Jerusalem. There were no mounts with me except the one I was riding on.

[13] By night, I went out through the Valley Gate toward the Jackal Well and the Dung Gate, examining the walls of Jerusalem, which had been broken down, and its gates, which had been destroyed by fire.

[14] Then I moved on toward the Fountain Gate and the King's Pool, but there was not enough room for my mount to get through;

[15,] so I went up the valley by night, examining the wall. Finally, I turned back and reentered through the Valley Gate.

[16] The officials did not know where I had gone or what I was doing because, as yet, I had said nothing to the Jews, the priests or nobles or officials, or any others who would be doing the work.

[17] Then I said to them, "You see the trouble we are in: Jerusalem lies in ruins, and its gates have been burned with fire. Come, let's rebuild the wall of Jerusalem, and we will no longer be in disgrace."

[18] I also told them about the gracious hand of my God on me and what the king had said to me. They replied, "Let us start rebuilding." So, they began this good work.

¹⁹ But when Sanballat the Horonite, Tobiah the Ammonite official and Geshem the Arab heard about it, they mocked and ridiculed us. "What is this you are doing?" they asked. "Are you rebelling against the king?"

²⁰ I answered them by saying, "The God of heaven will give us success. We, his ser ants, will start rebuilding, but as for you, you have no share in Jerusalem or any claim or historic right to it."

STUDY QUESTIONS FOR MEDITATION, REFLECTION AND ACTION

THEOLOGICAL MOMENT

- What about the work that caused Nehemiah to set a time or period to be silent and a time to speak to fellow Jews about the current status of Jerusalem?
- Why did the people who had no mind or thought of working become so interested in working?

PREACHING/TEACHING LENS

- Why should leaders motivate people?
- Can much be done by people in an organization without motivation from the Leader?

PERSONAL REFLECTION

- Are you a motivation for your team?
- In what ways have you motivated your team?
- What has been your experience?

COMMUNITY OUTLOOK

- What are some of the ways you intend to Motivate your community?
- Are there needs within your community that seem unnoticed?
- Are there unfinished projects that have been forgotten?
- In what way, or ways are you willing to motivate others to work?

CHAPTER 5

---ॐ---

THE FIFTH ESSENTIAL CHARACTERISTICS OF LEADERSHIP: THE LEADER'S ABILITY TO ORGANIZE THE WORK

Liberian Proverbs:
"GOOD PLAYER DON'T FIGHT FOR JERSEY."
People who know your worth will look for you when you are good.
"SARBEE (KNOWS HIS STUFF) NOT GO WORRY."
If you know your stuff, you don't have to worry;
people will find you.

Introduction

As the people of Liberia look forward to a new day, a new renaissance, and a new dispensation in the Nation and the Church, the people of Liberia must begin today, now, to hold the next batch of leaders they elect all over the country to new standards of accountability and leadership so that even when the leaders of the nation change from one election circle to another every six or nine years, the standards of leadership wouldn't change but get better.

Throughout this sermon series, I hope that leaders and people hold each other accountable to new leadership standards. I also hope that the people of Liberia will break the molds of the status quo, the old Liberian way, and begin a new day and a new way of leading.

Are you with me? Listen, whether you lead at home, in the neighborhood, in the community, in civil society, in business, in an institution, in the Church, or in the state, the people will take to heart Nehemiah's examples and become 360-degree leaders.

A burden was born inside of Nehemiah; he knew what God had called him to do; a king was won - with God's help, Nehemiah influenced other leaders higher than himself; a midnight moon-lite ride was taken - Nehemiah knew how to assess and examine the situation he was faced with; a speech was given by Nehemiah that motivated, and inspired the people of Jerusalem and made the people ready to rebuild the walls of Jerusalem. Shortly after his arrival in Jerusalem, Nehemiah is busy at work, putting the right people in the right places to get the work done the right way.

In this chapter, Nehemiah shares some helpful admonition with us as a people and a nation looking for a new kind of leadership in today's message. He shares three things about the Leader's ability to organize the work: the plan, The People, and the Places.

THE PLAN: The Leader Must Know How To Divide and Delegate the Work (vv. 1-5).

Division and delegation are important to accomplishing what God had called Nehemiah to do. Nehemiah chapters 1-2 report that upon Nehemiah's return to Jerusalem, he discovered the poor condition of the city's defenses. Immediately following is a list of those who worked on the wall, anticipating the work and the re-dedication that would come. He was a leader who wanted to make a difference for the glory of God.

Thomas Jefferson, in an 1801 letter to the merchants of New Haven, Connecticut, said, "of the various Executive duties, no one excites more anxious concern than that of placing the interests of our fellow citizens in the land of honest men, with understanding sufficient for their station no duty, at the same time is more difficult to fulfill."[24] The first part of Nehemiah's plan was to break the job down into smaller manageable units. The text tells us that Nehemiah has specific people who are the builders of the walls and specific gates. Nehemiah

---

[24] Jefferson to the New Haven Merchants, July 12, 1801, in PTJ, 34:554. Press copy available online from the Library of Congress. Transcription is available at Founders Online. The source of the above-mentioned paraphrase, which has been mistaken for a direct quote, is John B. McMaster's History of the People of the United States, which describes Jefferson's statement as follows: "Jefferson's reply to the remonstrance was a discussion of the tenure of office and soon forgotten. But one sentence will undoubtedly be remembered till our Republic ceases to exist. No duty the Executive ceases to exist. No duty the Executive had to perform was so trying he observed as to put the right man in the right place" John Bach McMaster. History of the People of the United States (New York: Appleton, 1921). 2:586.

placed them in stations according to their gifts and interests and had them build the portion of the wall right in front of their homes. He divided the wall, which was about a mile and a half long, into sections. So, assuming it was split evenly, each section was about 65 yards long. We noticed in v. 1 that the work of rebuilding the walls of Jerusalem was an organized work, with the leadership taking the lead and the people cooperating and following the leadership.

In chapter three of Nehemiah, we see impressive evidence of his organizational and administrative skills and how the widespread support for the wall-building project. All community segments cooperated with Nehemiah, supported the project, and completed the work. He was able and willing to work with all the structures of society. Forty-two groups of people are listed in this work of rebuilding the walls of Jerusalem. Each person had an area of responsibility, and God noticed each worker and put each person's name in the text.

According to John Maxwell, Nehemiah recognized the principles that make organizations progress—motivation with organization minus frustration. Leaders love everybody but move with the movers. Good organizations establish clear lines of authority. People do what you inspect and not what you expect. Leaders provide a supportive climate of trust and teamwork. Successful organizations recognize and reward effort. He was fine with delegating responsibility. He let go without letting up. He was not a micromanager. He definitely saw the project through, but not as a control freak. Nehemiah possessed tremendous faith in the people, and each person was assigned an area of responsibility.[25]

Are you with me? Listen, while it is true that no one person can do everything, like Nehemiah, the next batch of leaders of this Nation must remember that everybody can contribute, and they must put a plan together that will involve all of God's people—everybody can do something! The ruling position, the opposition, and the no position must come together to make a change."

Listen, Church, listen, Liberia. The task of rebuilding the walls of Jerusalem is everybody's responsibility for the work of this Nation going forward. God has gifted every child of God, and every Liberian contributes something – and God is interested in both our capability and our "availability as we work together to build a better nation. Then, he was fine with delegating responsibility. He let go without letting up. He was not a micromanager. He definitely saw the project through, but not as a control freak.

Are you with me? Listen, in v.5, like in the days of Nehemiah, God reminds us that there are and will be some people who will "refuse to get involved in the work." How sad!

The leaders we elect must have a plan, the ability to divide and delegate work, and a grasp of leadership that includes knowing the importance of delegation and choosing assistants with care.

---

[25] John Maxwell. The Maxwell Leadership Bible. pp. 580-581.

THE PEOPLE:
Everybody Contributes to the Work (VV. 6-12).

Even though God and the Temple are not mentioned, there are no sacrifices offered, no hymns sung, and no prayers said; we observe in the list of people mentioned how God and Nehemiah work with people from every segment of society to fully realize God's divine plans and promises for Jerusalem. Nehemiah's leadership is clear, without his name ever being mentioned and without his having to tout his own accomplishments.[26] I believe the real difference between a leader's success and failure, as exhibited by Nehemiah, can be very often traced to how that Leader brings out the great energies and talents of the people around him or her and gets the right people on board. Much of our impact as leaders is through others with the best talents and the right skills. [27]

Throughout this passage, we find that there is a variety of workers. This list of people working shows that all kinds of people are included and encouraged to get the work done. We see priests in verse 1, rulers in verses 12-19, and Craftsmen in verses 8-32. There were even Jews from other cities (vv. 2,5, &7). There were people from the

---

[26] The New Interpreter's Bible Commentary. Vol. III. Abingdon Press. pp. 770-771.

[27] Ron Ashkenas & Brook Manville. Harvard Business Review Leader's Handbook: Make An Impact, Inspire Your Organization, and Get to the Next Level. Harvard Business Review Press. Boston, Massachusetts. p.77. In chapter 3 of this book, Thomas J. Watson, Jr. is quoted as saying: "I believe the real difference between success and failure in a corporation can be very often traced to how well the organization brings out the great energies and talents of its people."

surrounding villages: tradesmen, city officials, women, bachelors, temple servants, city police, and merchants. Listen, Church, we should note that some people were willing to do more than required (vv. 11, 19, 21, 24, 27, & 30). And Nehemiah wisely positioned them to work near spots where they had a vested interest. He put the priests to work at the Sheep Gate, had people at work around their homes, police near the citadel, and governors near their offices. Therefore, they worked harder and better and lost less time in transit. And it worked so well that several groups did another section.

Every Leader at every level needs to have a top-notch team to help execute strategy, drive the organization forward, and implement the Leader's vision. Nehemiah is no exception. He recruited and inherited most of the team already in place to fulfill their particular roles and collaborate with others as needed in order to achieve the project's goal of rebuilding the wall. Finding people who meet the Leader's criteria doesn't mean that all those who work with and report to the Leader must look, act, or even think alike. Recruiting people around you with complementary and diverse skills is equally important. As a leader like Nehemiah, you must mix and match talents, backgrounds, and tendencies to allow the team to succeed collectively. Therefore, as you build your team, you must assess the current strength and background to give you a mix of people who are different enough to spark creative thoughts but can still collaborate and accomplish the task.[28]

Another small note that Nehemiah gives us is that he was an encourager. The whole community participated; the task was, in fact, completed. Like Nehemiah, going forward, we need leadership that knows how to delegate and inspire everybody at every level to contribute what they have to make the change we need happen.

THE PLACES: Everywhere was Important and needs the Leader's attention (vv. 6-30).

Because of the assessment Nehemiah did of the walls earlier, he identified the problems, put together a plan, and inspired the people. Now, he had to pay attention and fix and repair the places in the walls that had problems. In addition to the places in the wall that needed repairs, there are ten gates listed by name in this text, and each one of them is important to rebuilding the wall of Jerusalem.

There are definite spiritual lessons for us as we examine rebuilding the gates in Jerusalem's walls. It is gracious of God to record for us in His Holy Word a marvelous picture of the Christian life in these gates, and each one of them is significant. First, the Sheep Gate (v. 32) is in the eastern half of the northern wall, next to a market solely for sacrificial sheep. This gate speaks of the "Sacrifice of Christ on the Cross." For without the sacrifice, there can be no salvation! John

---

[28] Ibid. pp. 82-83.

says in 1:29, "Behold, the Lamb of God, which takes away the sin of the world." In chapter 10, verses 1-18, we notice no locks or bars on the Sheep Gate. The door of salvation is ever open to all of us who will be saved! Also, this is the only gate sanctified, setting it apart from all others as a special gate.

Second, the Fish Gate (vv.3-5) is named after the fish market in the immediate vicinity. It speaks of the work of believers as "soul-winners." In Mark 1:16-18 God commissioned all followers of Christ to be "fishers of me" and to communicate the Good News of Salvation to a lost and dying world. There is no greater privilege in all of the world than to be an "Ambassador of Christ."

Third, the Old Gate (vv.6-12) speaks of the importance of the "old path and old truths of the Word of God (Jer. 6:16). It seems like this world is ever looking for new ways (Acts 17:21). Listen, there is "no other way but Christ and His Cross. He is the answer to the world's woes.

Fourth, the Valley Gate (v. 13). It speaks of our "humility before the Lord." Just as Christ "humbled Himself and became flesh" so that He might save others, we should be willing, even in our leadership, to deny ourselves and minister to others. Sometimes, God allows us to go through the valley to prepare us for a future task, sometimes in order that we might be stronger now, and sometimes to get our attention. However, we have God's promise that "He will go through the valleys with us!"

Fifth is the Dung Gate (v. 14). This gate speaks of the necessity for the believer to constantly examine his own life to rid himself or herself of unconfessed sins! It was through The Dung Gate that waste and refuse were taken and cast into a fire. Imagine how difficult it would be to repair such a gate as this . . . yet we have the promise of God that states, "If we confess our sins, He is faithful and just to forgive us our sins and cleanse us from all unrighteousness." This was a very important gate to the city of Jerusalem, and it is a fundamental principle for believers and leaders today! (2 Cor. 7:1).

Six, the Gate of the Fountain (vv. 15-25) illustrates the ministry of the Holy Spirit. Today, the Holy Spirit binds believers together so that we might see the work accomplished.

It is also interesting to note the sequence of the last three gates mentioned: the Valley Gate (humility), the Dung Gate (cleansing), and the Gate of the Fountain (filling of the Spirit). Before we can access the power within us, we must exercise humility, confess our sins, and be filled (controlled) by the Holy Spirit!

Seventh, the Water Gate (v. 27). It speaks of the Word of God. This gate was used to bring water into the city – An aqueduct brought some water into the city, but not all of it. The remainder was carried in through the water gate. Often, God's Word refers to itself as "water" (Eph. 5:26; Ps. 119:9). It is also important to note that this is the only gate that needs "NO REPAIRS!"

Eight, the Horse Gate (v. 28) speaks of the "believer's warfare". The horse was the animal ridden by a warrior! Believers are engaged in "spiritual warfare!" (Eph. 6:10-18; 2 Timothy 2:3-4). There are many adversaries of the believer, and leaders must be prepared for battle on a daily basis. Paul wrote to the Corinthians, "For a great door and effectual is opened unto me, and there are many adversaries." (1 Cor. 16:19)

Nine, the East Gate (vv. 29-30). This gate is perhaps the most well-known gate of them all. It fills the student of God's Word with enthusiasm and excitement because of its connection with the second coming of Christ. This was the first gate opened in the morning.

The ten gates is the Miphkah gate. It speaks of judgment. The word "Miphkad" actually means in Hebrew review, registry, appointment, account, census, mustering. In the days of David, the soldiers would pass through this gate "in review" before their king, who stood to greet them and express his gratitude for their unselfish loyalty and daring. It was also a gate in which those who entered the city had to "register." Whether or not a person is saved, "we must ALL give an account of ourselves before the Lord" (Rom. 14:12). We cannot escape the Judgment of God (Hebrews 9:27). Therefore, everyone ought to give earnest heed; prepare to meet your God (Amos 4:12).

As we seek to rebuild, renew, clean, and set this Nation on a new path, the next batch of leaders we elect must realize that everyone and everywhere is important and needs our attention. In the words of songwriter and singer Junior Freeman and African Soldier, "Da My Area (Dumyarea). Everybody got to their area. Some people got their area to make market. Some people got their area to lead. Your area is your area, and my area is my area."[29]. Everyone has something to offer to bring the change and transformation the Nation needs.

Are you with me? Listen, Nehemiah organized the work. He got the whole community to participate. The task of rebuilding the wall was, in fact, completed. Listen, we know the outcome of Nehemiah's mission before he tells us about it. God's grace and the kindness of leaders with more influence than Nehemiah enabled him and all kinds of people to rebuild the walls of Jerusalem. All attempts to stop Nehemiah were useless.

Like Nehemiah, going forward, we need a new kind of leadership with impressive evidence of organizational and administrative skills. A new kind of leadership that is able and willing to work with people from every segment of the community and society structures to fully realize God's plans and promises for the Nation.

To the next batch of leaders we elect, listen. Going forward, I say to you, don't be overwhelmed by the size of the work you have been called and elected to do. Plan your work. Secondly, don't try to do the work along. Everywhere and everyone is important; inspire people to help. Lastly, don't do anything without including God. Put everything you do in prayer, and consecrate your tasks to the Lord. And listen, success without God is not success at all.

---

[29] Junior Freeman and African Soldier are Liberian Artists who wrote the famous Liberian song: THAT MY AREA.

CASE STUDIES

TO ORGANIZE

> To plan your work and activities in a coherent, orderly, and efficiently functioning whole.

LEADING DOWN

> The Fifth Essential Character of Leadership: The Leader's Ability to Organize the Work.
>
> Read the following case studies from the scriptures below and answer the following study questions.

PRAYER TEXT:

NEHEMIAH 3:1-32: BUILDERS OF THE WALL

¹ Eliashib, the high priest, and his fellow priests went to work and rebuilt the Sheep Gate. They dedicated it and set its doors in place, building as far as the Tower of the Hundred, which they dedicated, and as far as the Tower of Hananel.

² The men of Jericho built the adjoining section, and Zakkur son of Imri built next to them.

³ The Fish Gate was rebuilt by the sons of Hassenaah. They laid its beams and put its doors and bolts and bars in place.

⁴ _Meremoth son of Uriah, the son of Hakkoz, repaired the next section. Next to him Meshullam son of Berekiah, the son of Meshezabel, made repairs, and next to him Zadok son of Baana also made repairs.

⁵ The next section was repaired by the men of Tekoa, but their nobles would not put their shoulders to the work under their supervisors.

⁶ The Jeshanah Gate was repaired by Joiada son of Paseah and Meshullam son of Besodeiah. They laid its beams and put its doors with their bolts and bars in place.

⁷ Next to them, repairs were made by men from Gibeon and Mizpah—Melatiah of Gibeon and Jadon of Meronoth—places under the authority of the governor of Trans-Euphrates.

⁸ Uzziel son of Harhaiah, one of the goldsmiths, repaired the next section; and Hananiah, one of the perfume-makers, made repairs next to that. They restored Jerusalem as far as the Broad Wall.

⁹ Rephaiah son of Hur, ruler of a half-district of Jerusalem, repaired the next section.

¹⁰ Adjoining this, Jedaiah son of Harumaph made repairs opposite his house, and Hattush son of Hashabneiah made repairs next to him.

¹¹ _Malkijah son of Harim and Hasshub son of Pahath-Moab repaired another section and the Tower of the Ovens.

¹² Shallum son of Hallohesh, ruler of a half-district of Jerusalem, repaired the next section with the help of his daughters.

¹³ The Valley Gate was repaired by Hanun and the residents of Zanoah. They rebuilt it and put its doors with their bolts and bars in place. They also repaired a thousand cubits of the wall as far as the Dung Gate.

¹⁴ The Dung Gate was repaired by Malkijah son of Rekab, ruler of the district of Beth Hakkerem. He rebuilt it and placed its doors with their bolts and bars.

¹⁵ The Fountain Gate was repaired by Shallun, son of Kol-Hozeh, ruler of the district of Mizpah. He rebuilt it, roofing it over and putting its doors and bolts and bars in place. He also repaired the wall of the Pool of Siloam by the King's Garden, as far as the steps going down from the City of David.

¹⁶ Beyond him, Nehemiah son of Azbuk, ruler of a half-district of Beth Zur, made repairs up to a point opposite the tombs of David, as far as the artificial pool and the House of the Heroes.

¹⁷ Next to him, the repairs were made by the Levites under Rehum son of Bani. Beside him, Hashabiah, ruler of half the district of Keilah, carried out repairs for his district.

¹⁸ Next to him, the repairs were made by their fellow Levites under Binnui, son of Henadad, ruler of the other half-district of Keilah.

¹⁹ Next to him, Ezer son of Jeshua, ruler of Mizpah, repaired another section, from a point facing the ascent to the armory as far as the angle of the wall.

²⁰ Next to him, Baruch son of Zabbai zealously repaired another section, from the angle to the entrance of the house of Eliashib the high priest.

²¹ Next to him, Meremoth son of Uriah, the son of Hakkoz, repaired another section, from the entrance of Eliashib's house to the end of it.

²² The repairs next to him were made by the priests from the surrounding region.

²³ Beyond them, Benjamin and Hasshub made repairs in front of their house; and next to them, Azariah son of Maaseiah, the son of Ananiah, made repairs beside his house.

²⁴ Next to him, Binnui, son of Henadad, repaired another section, from Azariah's house to the angle and the corner,

²⁵ and Palal son of Uzai worked opposite the angle and the tower projecting from the upper palace near the court of the guard. Next to him, Pedaiah son of Parosh

²⁶ and the temple servants living on the hill of Ophel made repairs up to a point opposite the Water Gate toward the east and the projecting tower.

²⁷ Next to them, the men of Tekoa repaired another section, from the great projecting tower to the wall of Ophel.

²⁸ Above the Horse Gate, the priests made repairs, each in front of his own house.

²⁹ Next to them, Zadok son of Immer made repairs opposite his house. Next to him, Shemaiah, son of Shekaniah, the guard at the East Gate, made repairs.

³⁰ Next to him, Hananiah son of Shelemiah, and Hanun, the sixth son of Zalaph, repaired another section. Next to them, Meshullam, son of Berekiah, made repairs opposite his living quarters.

³¹ Next to him, Malkijah, one of the goldsmiths, made repairs as far as the house of the temple servants and the merchants, opposite the Inspection Gate, and as far as the room above the corner;

³² and between the room above the corner and the Sheep Gate the goldsmiths and merchants made repairs.

STUDY QUESTIONS FOR MEDITATION, REFLECTION AND ACTION

THEOLOGICAL MOMENT

- I want you to consider how and why the work was divided into various sessions.
- Are there advantages when the Leader organizes the work?
- Why were different people given different tasks?

PREACHING/TEACHING LENS

- What kind of work do you have to do as a leader?
- How do you go about carrying out the task that God has called you to do?
- Do you organize your work and give different people different responsibilities; are there set timelines for completion?

PERSONAL REFLECTION

- What would you say is your strength in organizing your work as a leader?
- Do you know the ability of your team members individually?
- In what area(s) do you need to improve in organizing your work?

COMMUNITY OUTLOOK

- Do you have a project or plan to conduct that will improve your community?
- Are there plans to divide the work into sessions?

LEADING LITERALLY

CHAPTER 6

THE SIX ESSENTIAL CHARACTERISTICS OF LEADERSHIP: THE LEADER'S ABILITY TO DEAL WITH OPPOSITION

Liberian Proverbs:
"AN EAGLE CAN FLY HIGH, BUT IT HAS TO COME
DOWN TO DRINK MUDDY WATER."
Be careful who you step on when you're going up; you may meet
the same person when you're coming down.
"IF YOU MAKE YOUR BED HARD, YOU WILL LIE ON IT HARD."
What you do now will determine your future.
"TAKE TIME IS BETTER THAN BEGGING PARDON
Be careful now, and you won't have to apologize later.
EVERYDAY PITCHER TO THE WELL, ONE DAY IT WILL BREAK."
You may get away with what you're doing now,
but you will be caught one day.

The leader with the ability to lead other leaders with equal influence and resources is a lateral (east and west) rial leader and a peer-to-peer leader. This distinguishes a competent leader from one who leads at the next level. This leader identifies, gathers, organizes, and puts to work followers. As hard as this may be, a leader who is only able to lead oneself and those below (south) is a limited leader. To lead at the next level, a leader must be able to lead other leaders above (north) and alongside them. Leading laterally is another kind of leadership, and it comes with a different type of challenge and is difficult.

To succeed as a 360-degree leader who leads laterally, you have to work at giving your peers; your equals, reasons to respect and follow you, even if they ignore you, disagree with you, or consider themselves your opponents.[30]

After the walls around Jerusalem started going up in chapter three, the word got around to Sanballat for the construction, reconstruction, and repairs. Sanballat and Tobiah (as we saw in 2:19) had a vested interest in Nehemiah's and Israel's failure and they began to organize the opposition. Are you with me? Listen, they knew that the repairs of the wall and the restoration of Jerusalem would bring a new day, a change, and a major shift in the city's commercial, spiritual, and political power. Sanballat Tobiah and the opposition were interested in how things have always been - in the status quo. Listen, church, listen, people of Liberia, those who have nothing to offer to bring change and transformation to the deplorable condition of the

---

[30] John Maxwell. The 360-Degree Leaders: Developing Your Influence From Anywhere in the Organization. Thomas Nelson Press. Nashville, Tennessee. 2005. pp.159-160.

Nation and its people, are always interested in things remaining the way they are.

In this chapter, we will explore the external opposition Nehemiah faced as he and the people of Jerusalem rebuilt the wall of Jerusalem. We will learn how to deal with the opposition. His stellar leadership in chapter 4 has some important lessons to teach us how to deal with the opposition. In this chapter, we will share three lessons every leader needs to learn about the opposition (Nehemiah 4:1-23). A more experienced leader once told me that you can only tell what a leader is made of when facing opposition. He said one of the great tests of leadership is how you handle opposition.

Listen, in life, and rebuilding for change and transformation, whether in business, marriage, church, or Nation, will bring out the opposition in others. In today's message, Nehemiah shows us that that's not necessarily bad. In fact, I might even say that if there is no opposition, either you are not rebuilding enough or changing enough, or people just don't care one way or the other. It doesn't matter who you are and where you lead you will face these challenges. Nehemiah identifies three lessons all of us - every Godly leader can learn from the opposition.

Opposition Is An Unavoidable By-Product of Obedience to God

As followers of Christ, we can and should expect opposition when we do what God calls us to do. Our obedience to God will trigger opposition from others who oppose it.

Listen, in their opposition, Sanballat and his friends mocked, ridiculed, insulted, and threatened Nehemiah and God's people. They offered compromising alliances and attempted to discourage and incite others against Nehemiah. They questioned his ability, his faith, and his motivation. They intimidated and accused Nehemiah unjustly.

Nehemiah had a great passion for the things of God, and he is a great example for us today. How a leader handles ridicule and insults tells us much about the leader. At some point in our lives, we will come face to face with opposition and problems; the question is how we will respond to them when they come. Notice what Nehemiah did and what he didn't do. Even though the work of rebuilding the wall was overwhelming, he didn't fire back a barrage of insults and harsh words. He went to prayer and kept doing the work of Him who had sent him.

Like Nehemiah, we need a new kind of leadership that does not act under the influence of anger and jealousy. The kind that takes the time to think things over. The kind that refuses to retaliate because the Lord says vengeance is mine, and I will repay. The kind that is sure their motivation is right and the glory of God and the furtherance of God's work are at stake, not just their wounded pride. We need a new kind of leadership that goes to God in prayer, trusting, and believing in obedience to the word of God. The kind that holds its peace and allows the Lord to fight its battle, victory shall surely be the leader. The type of leader that moves ahead with the work that God has planned for them and trusts God to show them how to overcome the obstacles.

As believers, we should expect opposition when we obey God, do his work, and work in alignment with his will for us. Our obedience to God will lead to unbelieving forces, be it spiritual or physical, working against us and God's will. The opposition may offer compromising alliances, or they may attempt to discourage and intimidate our efforts or accuse us unjustly. These are tactics of the opposition, and they shouldn't halt us. In spite of the opposition, we must learn to always move ahead with the work God has planned for us and trust him to show us how to overcome and handle the opposition.

If there is one thing that the Devil hates the most, it is the people of God, followers of Christ, who are walking in obedience to God. Therefore, I say to God's people and tomorrow's leaders, move ahead with the work that God has planned for us (in this Nation) and trust him to show us how to overcome our obstacles.

The Opposition Is An Opportunity To Show Strength of Character

Opposition should show you what you are made of if God calls you to do what you do. When Sanballat and his compromising alliances realized that demoralization, ridicule, and insults were not working, they introduced resistance and threats. They recruited a surrounding force and began to plan and launch violent attacks against the workers on every side. Usually, those who really oppose the work of God have no problem turning to violence to thwart the plan of God. Prayer must always be our first option when we are threatened by violence.

We must also take practical steps to protect ourselves and the people in our institution or Nation, which God has assigned us to lead. But remember, there are no guarantees of protection for Christians. Therefore, much like with ridicule, you forgive and move on with the assigned task and responsibility.

At this point, the wall was halfway completed, the people became weary and worried, and it wasn't easy. The people became weary and worried. The concern came from those who dealt too close to the enemy. So, Nehemiah reorganized the people into family fighting groups, which was the traditional way to do things in Israel. He moved the people away from the enemy and reminded them of their motivation. He encouraged them to remember that the Lord will be glorified in their generation.

He inspired them to turn their attention back to the work and continue to stand on God's promises, the Lord strong and mighty. He told them to stop being afraid because God always fights on their behalf. He reminded them of their priority of finishing the wall and bringing change and transformation to the Nation.

At this point, when the opposition threatened Nehemiah, the strength of his character was seen; he did not run from the opposition; he didn't retaliate evil for evil or violence for violence against the opposition. Listen, after he prayed, he went back to work. He didn't stop the construction. He posted guards to help watch for sneak attacks and stop the plans of the enemy. When problems arose, Nehemiah did not question God. Nehemiah went on his knees and prayed. He faced and overcame the opposition. Sometimes, when you go to do the work of God, he will allow your faith to be tested to see what you are made of.

Listen, leaders of tomorrow, when you face the opposition, remember that prayer is the most underused defense and the most significant weapon against the opposition. As a friend, a coach, a worker, a teacher, or the president of the Nation, remember the Lord. Prayer is the key. Meditate on the glory of the Lord and rely on his strength and power. The way to deal with the opposition is to show them your strength of character.

The Opposition Sometimes Reveals People's Fear of Change:

Listen, not everybody wants change. Not everyone wants things to get better. This is about the third time that we have seen and heard from Sanballat and his crew and their opposition to Nehemiah and the reconstruction of the wall. It is clear that Sanballat and his friends were afraid of and were against the change that was on the way to Jerusalem with the reconstruction of the wall. Sanballat's first reaction was anger. Why would someone get angry when someone else is being constructive and productive? Fear of others and of the accomplishment of others brings ridicule. Sanballat and others like him feared the coming change; they wanted things to stay the same and did not want Jerusalem to be rebuilt. The reality was that Sanballat was a neighboring official who knew that if Jerusalem was rebuilt, he might just lose power.

After the walls around Jerusalem started going up in chapter three, the word got around to Sanballat for the construction, reconstruction, and repairs. Sanballat and Tobiah (also in 2:19) had a vested interest in Nehemiah's and Israel's failure, and they began to organize the opposition. Are you with me? Listen, they knew that the repairs and reconstruction of the walls and the restoration of Jerusalem would bring a change, a new day, and a major shift in the Nation's commercial, spiritual, and political power.

Listen, just like Sanballat, Tobiah, and their crew, there are those today who are interested in the way things have always been. Why, Pastor Sam, I am glad you ask. Because change will expose the fact that they have nothing to offer when things are better.

Listen, church, listen. The people of Liberia, those with nothing to offer to bring change and transformation to the Nation's deplorable conditions, are always interested in things remaining the way they are. They say to us, "Don't change just for change's sake."

As we move into the second round of our elections, we notice various compromising alliances forming. Just like Sanballot and his friends, there are those who do not want to see a new day and a new kind of leadership in this Nation, so they resort to ridicule, insults, resistance, and threats. There are folks out there who can't succeed when we do well. There are folks who only succeed and profit when things are not going well, the economy is bad, the city is dirty, insecurity and poverty are on the rise, and the physical and spiritual walls of the Nation are destroyed. there is ruin. When things are going well, they have nothing to offer. There are Sanballots and Tobiahs on the land. Listen, church, listen, Liberia; there are those out there who are threatened by the change on the way.

Nehemiah didn't go to Jerusalem to fight. He went to build the wall, and he refused to get sidetracked, even by death threats. Like all leaders, he faced opposition. Today, we have seen what made Nehemiah a great leader. We can emulate these principles, even in the face of criticism; we will keep our hearts filled with faith and our focus securely on Jesus Christ.

CASE STUDIES

THE OPPOSITION

> The driving force behind human action is filled with energy and enthusiasm to work with high commitment.

LEADING LATERALLY

> The Sixth Essential Character of Leadership: The Leader's Ability to Handle the Opposition.
>
> Read these Bible case studies below and answer the following study questions.

PRAYER TEXT:

NEHEMIAH 4:1-23: OPPOSITION TO THE REBUILDING

1. When Sanballat heard that we were rebuilding the wall, he became angry and was greatly incensed. He ridiculed the Jews,

2. and in the presence of his associates and the army of Samaria, he said, "What are those feeble Jews doing? Will they restore their wall? Will they offer sacrifices? Will they finish in a day? Can they bring the stones back to life from those heaps of rubble—burned as they are?"

^{3.} Tobiah the Ammonite, who was at his side, said, "What they are building—even a fox climbing up on it would break down their wall of stones!"

^{4.} Hear us, our God, for we are despised. Turn their insults back on their own heads. Give them over as plunder in a land of captivity.

^{5.} Do not cover up their guilt or blot out their sins from your sight, for they have thrown insults in the face of the builders.

^{6.} So we rebuilt the wall till all of it reached half its height, for the people worked with all their heart.

^{7.} But when Sanballat, Tobiah, the Arabs, the Ammonites, and the people of Ashdod heard that the repairs to Jerusalem's walls had gone ahead and that the gaps were being closed, they were very angry.

^{8.} They all plotted together to come and fight against Jerusalem and stir up trouble against it.

^{9.} But we prayed to our God and posted a guard day and night to meet this threat.

^{10.} Meanwhile, the people in Judah said, "The strength of the laborers is giving out, and there is so much rubble that we cannot rebuild the wall."

^{11.} Also our enemies said, "Before they know it or see us, we will be right there among them and will kill them and put an end to the work."

^{12.} Then the Jews who lived near them came and told us ten times over, "Wherever you turn, they will attack us."

^{13.} Therefore I stationed some of the people behind the lowest points of the wall at the exposed places, posting them by families, with their swords, spears, and bows.

^{14.} After I looked things over, I stood up and said to the nobles, the officials, and the rest of the people, "Don't be afraid of them. Remember the Lord, who is great and awesome, and fight for your families, your sons and your daughters, your wives, and your homes."

^{15.} When our enemies heard that we were aware of their plot and that God had frustrated it, we all returned to the wall, each to our own work.

^{16.} From that day on, half of my men did the work, while the other half were equipped with spears, shields, bows, and armor. The officers posted themselves behind all the people of Judah

^{17.} who were building the wall. Those who carried materials did their work with one hand and held a weapon in the other,

^{18.} and each of the builders wore his sword at his side as he worked. But the man who sounded the trumpet stayed with me.

^{19.} Then I said to the nobles, the officials, and the rest of the people, "The work is extensive and spread out, and we are widely separated from each other along the wall.

^{20.} Wherever you hear the sound of the trumpet, join us there. Our God will fight for us!"

^{21.} So we continued the work with half the men holding spears from the first light of dawn till the stars came out.

^{22.} At that time I also said to the people, "Have every man and his helper stay inside Jerusalem at night, so they can serve us as guards by night and as workers by day."

^{23.} Neither I nor my brothers nor my men nor the guards with me took off our clothes; each had his weapon, even when he went for water.

STUDY QUESTIONS FOR MEDITATION, REFLECTION AND ACTION

THEOLOGICAL MOMENT

- Why was Nehemiah so focused on his job and never gave his time to listen to the opposition?
- Why, at no point in time, did Nehemiah report or pray against the opposition?
- Why did Nehemiah plant men at various Points to watch while the work was underway?
- What wrong did Nehemiah do that caused the opposition to fight him?

PREACHING/TEACHING LENS

- How well do you keep your focus on the task assigned?
- How often do you pray to God when faced with opposition on the assigned work?
- Do you assign people at different levels of your work by involving everyone?

PERSONAL REFLECTION

- What is your strength in sharing tasks as a leader? How well do you understand your team of workers as a leader?
- In what areas are you to improve in distributing tasks at work?
- Are you focused on the task that oppositions will not get you off it?
- Was there any time you could not complete a task because of opposition?
- Was there any time in your leadership that you completed a project amid opposition?

COMMUNITY OUTLOOK

- In what way are you going to help people in dealing with the opposition?
- What has been the story or challenges with opposition in your community?

CHAPTER 7

LEAVE IT BETTER THAN YOU MET IT: A JOB WELL DONE

Liberian Proverbs:
"THE SAME CLOCK THAT STRIKES MIDNIGHT STRIKES MIDDAY."
Things may be challenging today, but they may be better
tomorrow.

African Proverb
"IF YOU THINK YOU ARE TOO SMALL TO MAKE A DIFFERENCE,
YOU HAVEN'T SPEND A NIGHT WITH A MOSQUITO."
One Person Can Make a Real Difference

One day, when our journey here on earth ends, we pray and hope that the Lord will say to each of us in Matthew 25:23, "Well done thy good and faithful servant." These words are some of the most appropriate descriptions of a marvelous testimony of a committed servant, a wonderful journey, and a job well done.

In this chapter, we will see the testimony of a job well done that gives us a wonderful picture of what happens when a leader, called by God, performs with excellence and commitment, completes the task, and leaves the assignment and the place the leader is called to serve better than the leader met it. This is a testimony of a job well done by Nehemiah, God's good and faithful servant.

Over the last seven chapters of the study of the life of Nehemiah, a servant to the King and a volunteer leader, this series of sermons has provided us with a wonderful study on leadership. Nehemiah, a layman called by God to lead in Jerusalem, shared with us several essential characteristics of leadership that have been useful in the process of learning how to select leaders generally and specifically in the October 10 and the November 14 presidential and legislative and run-off elections respectively for new leaders in Liberia, West African. Nehemiah led himself (self-leadership), sure of God's call to leave the King's palace in Shushan, sacrifice his comfort, and lead God's people in Jerusalem. Nehemiah led (Leading up) the King. He influenced leaders more powerful and resourceful than he, and by God's grace, he received the resources he needed to carry out and complete God's assignment in Jerusalem; Nehemiah led (leading down) God's people who followed him. He motivated and inspired them to come together, work together, and achieve God's purpose for their lives. For the Nation, Nehemiah led (leading laterally) his peers, his equals, and the opposition and finished strong. Nehemiah cared for the work God called him to do. He prayed for help. He motivated and inspired the followers. He organized the work, and He taught us lessons from the opposition.

After dealing with some external conflict against the work of rebuilding the walls and taking some time off to call a community meeting to deal with internal conflict, Nehemiah is nearing the end of completing his assignment. So, the attacks against Nehemiah become much more personal. But when the going gets tough, and the going gets tough, Nehemiah trusted God, was committed to the assignment, and completed the work in Jerusalem. He left the city better than he met it.

Like Nehemiah, we need leaders today who know how to finish strong and leave the place God assigned them better than they met it. Are you with me? Listen church, in a generation where leaders are quitters, church hoppers, self-centered, never finishers, complainers, status quo advocates instead of agents of change, creators of problems instead of finders of solutions, the church, civil society, institutions, organizations, and the Nation needs leaders with a new kind of leadership that will commit to selfless service, others-centered, institution before individual, a new type of leadership that knows how to endure to the end, finishes well, and always leave the place better than it met it.

In this closing chapter of this series, Nehemiah teaches us that sometimes, when others attack and oppose us and have nothing good to say about us and what we try to do, it is meant to deflect attention from their own faults, failures, and inability to deliver and produce anything good. How do you know this, Pastor Sam? I am glad you asked Dr. Angeline Benson. Sanballat charged Nehemiah and the Jews with plotting rebellion (6:6). Still, in fact, Sanballat and his crew were plotting to harm Nehemiah (6:2). Sanballat accused Nehemiah of hiring prophets to further his own royal ambition (6:7). Still, in fact, Tobiah and Sanballat themselves had hired a prophet of God, Shemaiah to discredit and compromise Nehemiah. Nehemiah tried several approaches to defend himself. He told them that he was too busy with the work on the wall he just couldn't get away (6:3). They told Nehemiah he had a message from God. Therefore, Nehemiah attended this meeting because he was godly and hoped to hear from God. But he realized from the advice that it was another trick (6:12) and flatly said no (6:8, & 11).

Nehemiah asked the Lord to return the deeds of Sanballat and Tobiah on their own heads (6:14) because he knew that vengeance belongs to the Lord. The opposition's trick to discourage Nehemiah and the workers only encouraged them (6:9). Like Jeremiah, Nehemiah knew he was not obligated to listen to a prophet whom God had not sent (6:12; Jer. 28:15-16). Listen, church; listen, leaders; not every prophet that comes your way is sent by God. Gold, not God, inspires some of them. They are hired by the opposition as prophets of falsehood.

As we close this special election sermon series on leadership, Nehemiah teaches us in this final message that whenever God gives you an assignment, God expects you to, and you must leave the assignment better than you encountered it. Leaders called by God are agents of change for good.

Nehemiah tells us the story of the completion and restoration of the walls of Jerusalem in only fifty-two days. He finished strong and left the place better than he found it. Nehemiah impacted the Nation, inspired the population, and took the city, the people, the condition, and the Nation to the next level. Things were much improved commercially, spiritually, and politically.

The walls in the south and the west of the city only needed repairing; he fixed them. The wall on the east was partially new, with some debris; he cleaned it up and painted it (Ezra 4:8-23). The walls in the north were rebuilt. The enthusiasm and commitment of Nehemiah, as well as the excitement and overwhelming cooperation of the people, also propelled the wall's completion. He finished strong; he left the place better than he saw it.

When those opposed to Nehemiah (Sanballat and his compromising alliances) heard about the wall's completion, they were scared, lost their self-confidence, and recognized the power of Nehemiah's God. Are you with me? Church, people of Liberia! When you hold your peace and let the Lord fight your battle, those who are opposed to what God calls you to do will, in God's own time, recognize, proclaim, and ascribe your success to the God who sent you. Listen, church; listen, people of Liberia! God got the glory for Nehemiah's successes. When that happens, Like Nehemiah, you have finished strong and left the place better than it was.

As we look forward to a new day, a new renaissance, and a new dispensation in every section of the Nation, Church, and people of Liberia, we must begin with the October 10 and November 14th elections to hold the next batch of legislative, and presidential leaders we elected, and will elect all over this country to new standards of accountability and leadership so that even when our leaders change from one election circle to another, the standards and value do not change but get better.

I pray and hope that the leaders and people will hold each other accountable to a new standard. And that we can break the mode of the status quo, the Liberian way, and begin a new day. Are you with me? Listen, whether you lead at home, in the neighborhood, in the community, in civil society, in a business, in an institution, in the marketplace, in the church, or in the state, you will take to heart the essential characteristics of Nehemiah and become a 360-degree leader, who is able to finish strong and leave the place better than you met it.

Going forward, we need leaders who will leave their assignments, positions, offices, organizations, institutions, and the Nation better than they met it. Leaders who will leave the streets cleaner than they met them; the economy in a better state than they found it; poor people in a better position than you met them; Sick people in a healthier condition than they discovered them; Handicapped people in a better state of improving their condition than they met them.

CASE STUDIES

COMMITMENT

> The driving force behind human action is filled with energy and enthusiasm to work with high commitment.

LEADING LATERALLY

> The Seventh Essential Character of Leadership: The Leader's Ability to Leave the Place Better than They Met It: A Job Well Done.
>
> Read these Bible case studies below and answer the following study questions.

PRAYER TEXT

NEHEMIAH 6:1-19: FURTHER OPPOSITION TO THE REBUILDING

1. When word came to Sanballat, Tobiah, Geshem the Arab, and the rest of our enemies that I had rebuilt the wall and not a gap was left in it—though up to that time I had not set the doors in the gates—

2. Sanballat and Geshem sent me this message: "Come, let us meet together in one of the villages on the plain of Ono." But they were scheming to harm me;

3. so I sent messengers to them with this reply: "I am carrying on a great project and cannot go down. Why should the work stop while I leave it and go down to you?"

4. Four times they sent me the same message, and each time I gave them the same answer.

5. Then, the fifth time, Sanballat sent his aide to me with the same message, and in his hand was an unsealed letter

6. in which was written: "It is reported among the nations—and Geshem says it is true—that you and the Jews are plotting to revolt, and therefore you are building the wall. Moreover, according to these reports, you are about to become their King,

7. and have even appointed prophets to make this proclamation about you in Jerusalem: 'There is a king in Judah!' Now this report will get back to the King; so, come, let us meet together."

8. I sent him this reply: "Nothing like what you are saying is happening; you are just making it up out of your head."

9. They were all trying to frighten us, thinking, "Their hands will get too weak for the work, and it will not be completed." But I prayed, "Now strengthen my hands."

10. One day I went to the house of Shemaiah son of Delaiah, the son of Mehetabel, who was shut in at his home. He said, "Let us meet in the house of God, inside the temple, and let us close the temple doors, because men are coming to kill you—by night they are coming to kill you."

11. But I said, "Should a man like me run away? Or should someone like me go into the temple to save his life? I will not go!"

¹². I realized that God had not sent him, but that he had prophesied against me because Tobiah and Sanballat had hired him.

¹³. He had been hired to intimidate me so that I would commit a sin by doing this, and then they would give me a bad name to discredit me.

¹⁴. Remember Tobiah and Sanballat, my God, because of what they have done; remember also the prophet Noadiah and how she and the rest of the prophets have been trying to intimidate me.

¹⁵. So the wall was completed on the twenty-fifth of Elul, in fifty-two days.

OPPOSITION TO THE COMPLETED WALL

¹⁶. When all our enemies heard about this, all the surrounding nations were afraid and lost their self-confidence, because they realized that this work had been done with the help of our God.

¹⁷. Also, in those days the nobles of Judah were sending many letters to Tobiah, and replies from Tobiah kept coming to them.

¹⁸. For many in Judah were under oath to him, since he was son-in-law to Shekaniah son of Arah, and his son Jehohanan had married the daughter of Meshullam son of Berekiah.

¹⁹. Moreover, they kept reporting to me his good deeds and then telling him what I said. And Tobiah sent letters to intimidate me.

STUDY QUESTIONS FOR MEDITATION, REFLECTION AND ACTION

THEOLOGICAL MOMENT

- Why was Nehemiah so firm in his decision not to respond to the call of the opposition?
- Why was the opposition so determined to distract Nehemiah from the work?
- Why was Nehemiah so focused on the Job that he could not have left it for anything?
- What if Nehemiah had left his task to focus on the opposition and their accusation?

PREACHING/TEACHING LENS

- Why was Nehemiah so particular about rebuilding the wall?
- Why was he so dependent on God to rebuild the wall?
- Why could he not give in to the opposition?
- Why was he willing to die for the betterment of the people of Jerusalem?

PERSONAL REFLECTION

- How well are you able to organize an institution for the better?
- How often do you run checks and balances on your assigned task?
- Do you assign people at different levels of your work by involving everyone?
- How did you leave the last office you occupied?
- How did you meet the new office you are occupying, and how do you intend to leave it?

COMMUNITY OUTLOOK

- What are your plans to make your community better than it is?
- Are there offices occupied in the community and left the same way they were?
- Are there programs you have to develop the leaders within your community to leave the office better than they will meet it?
- Name of few.

CHAPTER 8

SIDEBAR:
BONUS SERMONS CONTRIBUTIONS

Thanks to the following pastors and church leaders from Liberia to North America to the Caribbean for their contributions to this chapter of sermons on leadership.

REV. MARIA S. P. SMITH

> Theme: "Jethro, The Visionary Leader"
> Text: Exodus 18:13-23

[13] The next day Moses took his seat to serve as judge for the people, and they stood around him from morning till evening. [14] When his father-in-law saw all that Moses was doing for the people, he said, "What is this you are doing for the people? Why do you alone sit as a judge while all these people stand around you from morning till evening?"

[15] Moses answered him, "Because the people come to me to seek God's will. [16] Whenever they have a dispute, it is brought to me,

and I decide between the parties and inform them of God's decrees and instructions."

[17] Moses' father-in-law replied, "What you are doing is not good. [18] You and these people who come to you will only wear yourselves out. The work is too heavy for you; you cannot handle it alone. [19] Listen now to me, and I will give you some advice, and may God be with you. You must be the people's representative before God and bring their disputes to him. [20] Teach them his decrees and instructions and show them the way they are to live and how they are to behave. [21] But select capable men from all the people—men who fear God, trustworthy men who hate dishonest gain—and appoint them as officials over thousands, hundreds, fifties and tens. [22] Have them serve as judges for the people at all times but have them bring every difficult case to you; the simple cases they can decide themselves. That will make your load lighter, because they will share it with you. [23] If you do this and God so commands, you will be able to stand the strain, and all these people will go home satisfied."

The book of Exodus speaks of the deliverance and exodus of the children of Israel from Egypt by the hand of God, how He entered into a covenant relationship with them and dwelt in their midst. Whenever God wants to do something on earth, He always finds a person to use. In the case of Israel, God found Moses, whom He trained, equipped, and empowered to lead His people.

At some point in time, Moses married Zipporah, Jethro's daughter. Moses left Zipporah and his children, Gershom and Eliezer, with his father-in-law when God told him to go and deliver the children of Israel from Egypt. When Moses had accomplished this task, Jethro decided to take Moses' wife and children back to him at the camp where they were staying. After sharing pleasantries with Moses and the elders, he decided to spend some time with them. During this time, Jethro saw the unhealthy leadership practice that Moses was carrying out—he alone did everything.

As a visionary leader, Jethro decided to advise Moses on the best and most profitable way to lead God's people. Against this backdrop, I will concentrate on two points in my speech: "Jethro, The Visionary Leader." Before we proceed, let us establish the premise of who a leader and a visionary leader are.

Who is a leader?

A leader sees how things can be improved and rallies people toward that vision. Leaders can work toward making their vision a reality while putting people first.

Who is a visionary leader? A visionary leader can look well beyond the present and see the potential and possibilities in the future.

1. A Visionary Leader Sees the Problem (v.13,17)

Moses went about his usual duties in managing the affairs of the people. On this day, his job was to mediate disputes and dispense justice when there was an issue between the Israelites. Moses sat all day with the people surrounding him, waiting for him to inquire of

131

God on their behalf. Jethro saw the problem—what it was doing to Moses and the people and spoke to him about the wisdom of training others to share the responsibility of governing.

No one can lead a group of people, church, organization, or institution alone. Leaders need to have people around them who can help them run the organization or institution effectively so that it can succeed and accomplish its vision.

Roy T. Bennett stated, "Great leaders create more leaders, not followers." Jethro, the visionary leader, saw the need for Moses to select godly men of integrity to take over most cases. Jethro suggested that several layers of these judges deal with minor disputes, meaning that only the major cases make their way to him. By doing this, Moses would not wear himself or the people out, and they would get justice more quickly.

Visionary leaders always look for the problem and find ways to resolve it, which leads us to Jethro's next step.

2. A Visionary Leader Provides the Solution

A visionary leader is one who sees a problem and provides the solution. In the case of Moses' predicament, Jethro provided the following solutions:

a) Develop a Team (v. 21)

"But select capable men from all the people—men who fear God, trustworthy men who hate dishonest gain—and appoint them as officials over thousands, hundreds, fifties and tens." The development of a team is very important in leadership. The leader is responsible for assembling various members or individuals to build an effective team. A leader cannot do the work alone, as Jethro told Moses. Because if they try it, they will wear themselves out.

Jesus carried out a perfect example of such practices. When He was about to begin His Ministry, we are told that He developed a team of twelve men with different skills and backgrounds to assist Him in accomplishing God's vision. Team development enables a leader to accomplish much with less effort and strength, which the team members provide. Every person brings a unique perspective matched with a unique skill set.

We see the potential of team development being exhibited here on Providence Hill. There are nine departments, and each department is headed by a director who oversees the day-to-day operations of the church work, thus enabling Pastor Sam to do less and more. Less in the sense that the directors take care of different aspects of the church work, and the Pastor deals with other matters that lead to more things being done.

b) Delegate Responsibilities (v. 22)

"Have them serve as judges for the people at all times but bring every difficult case to you; the simple cases they can decide themselves. That will make your load lighter, because they will share it with you." Jethro told Moses not only to develop a team but also to delegate responsibilities to them.

133

Delegation is to give a particular job, duty, right, etc., to someone else so that they do it for you. Task delegation allows you to strategize more effectively. Without delegation, you might spend time completing several minor tasks, which may prevent you from prioritizing larger activities, as seen in the case of Moses. Task delegation provides you with more time to focus on complex tasks.

Jethro told Moses to delegate the task of judging the people at all times (to those that were selected), and where there were difficult cases they could not handle, they were to transfer them to him. This provided Moses with the opportunity to be the people's representative before God and bring their disputes to Him, to teach them His decrees and instructions, and to show them the way they were to live and how they were to behave. Moses was also able to stand the strain and

all the people went home satisfied in the end.

Finally, as leaders, we must learn to see the problem, develop a team that will help us solve it, and delegate responsibilities to team leaders. When that is done, the church, organization, or institution will grow to accomplish greater works.

Let Jesus Christ be praised!!![31]

---

[31] Rev. Atny Maria P. S. Smith, Director, Department of Christian Education Providence Baptist Church

Rev. Maria-Salome P. Smith was born from the union of Mr. and Mrs. Cosme R. Ellen Y. Pulano Sr. and is the oldest of four children. Maria is happily married to Bishop Lionel M. Smith, and their union has been blessed with four children (three biological and one adopted) and a granddaughter.

She graduated with a Bachelor of Religious Education (BRE) Degree in Christian Education from the Liberia Baptist Theological Seminary in 2006, a 2017 graduate

REV. DR. JOHN (CHIP) SLOANE

Theme: THE MINDSET OF A SERVANT LEADER

Doulos Servants

Text: Isaiah 6:1-9

"Ni da wouun hwedein ni, oh nyu tonon: Water becomes saliva when it remains in the mouth too long."- (Bassa Tribe, Liberian Proverb)

There are many words that ought to be used over and over in the church of Jesus Christ. Indeed, they ought to be featured in every Lord's Day worship service. Words like:

Cross - Paul preached a cross-centered gospel. He wrote to the church in Corinth, "For the message of the cross is foolishness to those who are perishing, but to us who are being saved it is the power of God" (1 Corinthians 1:18). For that reason, Paul explained that he did

---

of the Princeton Theological Seminary with a Master of Arts (MACEF) Degree in Christian Education and formation, and a 2022 graduate of the Louis Arthur Grimes School of Law with a Bachelor of Arts Degree in Law (LLB). She is a licensed lawyer of the Liberia National Bar Association (LNBA).

She runs an NGO called The Empowerment Teaching Ministry & Legal Clinic (ETM&LC), which is geared towards helping pre-trial detainees get due process by providing them with the best legal representation they will need. It also equips Ministers of the Gospel and church leaders with the legal knowledge that will empower them to help their congregations.

Rev. Smith was ordained as a Minister of the Gospel on February 19, 2012. She is currently the Director of Christian Education at Providence Baptist Church. In 2023, the congregation at Providence chose her as the Mother of the Year 2023/2024. She loves the Lord and earnestly desires to serve God with all her heart and be all that God has called her to be.

not go to Corinth relying on the eloquence of speech or human wisdom. He resolved to rely solely on and proclaim only the message of Jesus Christ and Him crucified (1 Corinthians 2:1-2). Like Paul, we ought to rally the church every Sunday around Jesus Christ and Him crucified. Resurrection – Sunday is the Lord's Day. It has been ever since the Sunday of His glorious resurrection. Every Sunday ought to be a reminder of the "living hope through the resurrection of Jesus Christ from the dead, and into an inheritance that can never perish, spoil or fade" (1 Peter 1:3-4).

Grace—Every blessing in Christ is by His grace. Grace is God doing for us what we could not do for ourselves, even when we do not deserve it. Grace is our motivation for what we do for Him. We may not sing John Newton's *Amazing Grace* every day or every Sunday, but we ought to appreciate His amazing grace daily.

After fifty-plus years of Ministry in the local church, I have come to believe that there is a word that should be used very sparingly. In fact, I'm trying to eliminate it from my vocabulary. It is difficult because it is so much a part of the church's vocabulary. The word that I want to limit (even omit) is *volunteer.*

Volunteer is not a Biblical word for Christians. We do not choose what we will do for the Lord or even if we will do anything. The closest that I can come is the call of Isaiah recorded in Isaiah 6.

In the year that King Uzziah died, I saw the Lord, high and exalted, seated on a throne, and the train of his robe filled the temple. [2] Above him were seraphim, each with six wings: With

136

two wings they covered their faces, with two they covered their feet, and with two they were flying. [3] And they were calling to one another:

"Holy, holy, holy is the *Lord* Almighty; the whole earth is full of his glory." [4.] At the sound of their voices, the doorposts and thresholds shook, and the temple was filled with smoke.

[5.] "Woe to me!" I cried. "I am ruined! For I am a man of unclean lips, and I live among a people of unclean lips, and my eyes have seen the King, the *Lord* Almighty."

[6.] Then one of the seraphim flew to me with a live coal in his hand, which he had taken with tongs from the altar. [7.] With it he touched my mouth and said, "See, this has touched your lips; your guilt is taken away and your sin atoned for."

[8.] Then I heard the voice of the Lord saying, "Whom shall I send? And who will go for us?" And I said, "Here am I. Send me!"

[9.] He said, "Go."

From John 12:41, we know it was Jesus, the pre-incarnate Christ, that Isaiah saw on the throne. It was Jesus who asked the question, "Whom shall I send? And who will go for us?" It was Isaiah who responded, "Here am I. Send me.!" It may sound like Isaiah was volunteering, but it was more than that. Isaiah is privileged to be granted this Heavenly vision. He is the lone human before the throne. The Lord asks him a rhetorical question. The answer is implied and expected. Isaiah is the one who is being called and the one who must answer. Jesus was not looking for a volunteer. He knew Isaiah's heart.

He knew Isaiah to be His servant. He called him; He commissioned him. In truth, the call was a command. The answer was expected and demanded.

I urge you to join me in the following Biblical and faithful confessions.

1. I am a servant.
2. I am a servant of the great and glorious Lord Jesus Christ.
3. I am a member of His church, the servant army.
4. I will be a servant leader.

1. I am a servant.

Paul, Timothy, James, Peter, and Jude all described themselves as "servants" of Christ (Romans 1:1; Philippians 1:1; James 1:1; 2 Peter 1:1; Jude 1:1). Actually, the word "servant" is less descriptive than the Greek word demands. The word used by these great followers of the Lord is *doulos*, meaning slave. It is not a word that we hold in high esteem today. It is a demeaning term by our standards. It means to be owned by someone.

We prefer to volunteer. It enables us to hold on to our dignity, our independence, our power. A volunteer may opt out of service but not a *doulos* servant. Jesus taught us to pray: "Our Father in Heaven, hallowed be Your name, Your kingdom come, Your will be done, on earth as it is in heaven." How is the Father's will done in Heaven? Immediately and completely! When God speaks to an angel in Heaven, the angel doesn't consider the cost of obedience to determine if it will accept the command. The angel simply obeys, immediately obeys and completely fulfills the task. For us to pray, the Lord's Prayer is to pray that we would be like the angels in obedience – doing God's will and obeying His commands wholly and immediately. That is what *doulos* servants do!

Will you make the confession – I am a servant?

2. I am a servant of the great and glorious Lord Jesus Christ.

Paul, Timothy, James, Peter, and Jude all claimed for themselves the title of *doulos* servant. They made the claim with the same pride as David in Psalm 23, when he wrote, "The Lord is my Shepherd." David lived in a world of sheep, flocks, and shepherds. He saw the good and bad shepherds. He stood before the world and announced proudly, "The LORD is MY SHEPHERD!" Of all the shepherds in the world, his shepherd was the best. I imagine Paul, Timothy, James, Peter, and Jude all making the same proud declaration. "The Lord is MY Master. The Lord Jesus Christ is MY owner. I am His. I am His servant."

There is nothing demeaning about being the *doulos* servant of the Lord Jesus Christ. In truth, there is joy and glory in the declaration – I am a servant of the great and glorious Lord Jesus Christ.

Will you make the confession – I am a servant of the great and glorious Lord Jesus Christ.

139

3. I am a member of His church, the servant army.

The Greek word for church is *ekklesia*, literally "called out ones." The church consists of people who have been called out of the world into Christ, out of sin into holiness, and out of self into service. Members of His church are not given the option of holiness and service, but holiness and service are characteristics of the "called out ones."

The church has often been described as a "voluntary army." That does not fit the Biblical description of the church of Jesus Christ, but perhaps it describes the church as we see it today. God commands His army to "Go and make disciples of all nations, baptizing them in the name of the Father, Son, and the Holy Spirit, and teaching them to obey everything I have commanded you." Many, if not most, respond, "Not now, send someone else." God commands His army to gather on Sunday for worship, but many say, "Not this Sunday, I have something else to do." God commands His army to give a tenth of their income to equip His army for His service, but many respond, "Not now; I have other commitments for my money."

A *doulos* servant does not have a choice in God's commands. It is His will that rules the servant's life. It is His day (Sunday, the Lord's Day), not the servant's day. It is His money, not the servant's money.

Will you make the confession – I am a member of His church, the servant army?

4. I will be a servant leader.

In counseling couples about marriage, I often share the following quote: "The only competition that ought to exist in a Christian marriage is the competition to outserve one another." That is also good advice for the church of the Lord Jesus Christ. That is a Biblical concept visible in the English Standard Version translation of Romans 12:9, which I believe is true to the original text, "Love one another with brotherly affection. <u>Outdo one another</u> in showing honor."

I hope you noticed a difference in the way I worded this last point.

I am a servant. That is my calling.

I am a servant of the great and glorious Lord Jesus Christ. He is great, and He is glorious. I am a member of His church, a servant army, not a volunteer army. Those are the facts, plain and simple. But the fourth and final statement deserves a more thoughtful and determined confession. I WILL BE a servant leader. Not only will I be a servant, but I will show how to be a servant. I will be the best servant of servants.

On the night of Jesus' betrayal, the night before His crucifixion, He celebrated the Passover meal with His disciples (servants). Entering the room, no disciple volunteered to serve by washing dirty feet. The bowl and the towel were there, but no disciples volunteered. Jesus Himself took the towel and bowl of water and washed the dirty feet. He became the servant and continued to be the servant leader. After washing the feet of the disciples, He said (John 13:15-17):

[15] I have set you an example that you should do as I have done for you. Very truly, I tell you, no servant is greater than his Master, nor is a messenger greater than the one who sent him. [17.] Now that you know these things, you will be blessed if you do them.

Today, the towel and bowl of water are present. The Lord Jesus is not asking for volunteers. He is commanding His servants to serve. He is commanding us to go forth in service. He is commanding us to set an example of being a *doulos* servant. He is commanding us to serve like Him. Will you make the confession—I WILL BE a servant leader?

Conclusion:

I began the sermon by saying that there are words that ought to be heard often, especially on the Lord's Day. These words call us to a life of servanthood.

Cross – Jesus said that He "did not come to be served but to serve and give

His life as a ransom for many" (Mark 10:45). Jesus served us at the cross; there, we find our motivation for service to God and others. The cross demands our lives, our all, be given in service.

"Do you not know that your bodies are temples of the Holy Spirit, who is in you, whom you have received from God? You are not your own;

you were bought at a price. Therefore, honor God with your bodies" (1 Corinthians 6:19-20).

Resurrection – 1 Corinthians 15 is known as the resurrection chapter. You hear the glorious affirmations –

12. "Christ has indeed been raised from the dead" (15:20);
"Death has been swallowed up in victory" (15:54);
"Thanks be to God! He gives us the victory through our
Lord Jesus Christ" (15:57).

The chapter ends with a call for us to serve.

"Therefore, my dear brothers and sisters, stand firm. Let nothing move you. Always give yourselves fully to the work of the Lord because you know that your labor in the Lord is not in vain" (15:58).

Grace – [11]"For the grace of God has appeared that offers salvation to all people. It teaches us to say "No" to ungodliness and worldly passions and to live self-controlled, upright, and godly lives in this present age, [13] while we wait for the blessed hope—the appearing of the glory of our great God and Savior, Jesus Christ, [15] who gave himself for us to redeem us from all wickedness and to purify for himself a people that are his very own, eager to do what is good" (Titus 2:11-14).

Grace teaches us to say "No" to the world and "Yes, of course, yes to the Lord." Grace teaches us that there is no shame in service, but there is glory to God in serving others. Will you make a good confession? – Jesus is Lord! Will you make the corresponding confessions:

I am a servant.

I am the servant of the great and glorious Lord Jesus Christ.

I am a member of the church of Jesus Christ, the servant army.

I WILL BE a servant leader.[32]

---

[32] Rev. Dr. John (Chip) Sloan is the Senior Pastor of the First Baptist Church in King's Mountain, North Carolina, United States of America.

Dr. John W. Sloan, Jr. (better known as Bro. Chip) is first and foremost a preacher of the unsearchable riches of Christ. His passion for Christ began as a freshman at Clemson University. There, he would have a life-transforming experience with Jesus Christ. Old things passed away, and everything became new in this new relationship with the Living God. Soon, the Lord revealed a calling to pastoral Ministry and Bro. Chip has been pursuing that calling ever since. By God's grace, Bro. Chip was given a partner in Ministry in Martha Doster. [They have been married for 53 years and have three children and four awesome grandchildren.]

To understand Bro. Chip's calling from the Lord, you have to go back to his days at New Orleans Baptist Theological Seminary. There, God impressed him with the need to reach the whole world with the saving Gospel of Jesus Christ. Bro. Chip and Martha assumed their role would be that of international missionaries. But God would clarify His calling in a missions class at the seminary taught by Dr. Helen Falls. From her, Bro. Chip learned the importance of being a "rope holder." William Carey, the Father of modern missions, committed to going to India. Carey is reported to have said to a group of like-minded supporters of foreign missions, "I will go down into the pit if you hold the rope." Later, Adoniram and Ann Judson would go down into the pit, and Luther Rice pledged to hold the rope. God plainly spoke to Bro. Chip and Martha to be "rope holders."

Bro. Chip's doctoral project was designed to lead a local congregation to mission support and action. Later, the Lord would enable Bro. Chip to lead First Baptist Kings Mountain to become a rope holding congregation. The Mission Readiness Program was established. Funds were provided in the yearly budget to send Church members on a mission at no cost to them but the cost of their passport. From that beginning, the Mission Readiness Program has sent hundreds of members on mission with the Gospel, established congregations in unreached areas, built church buildings, and contributed hundreds of thousands of dollars to support missionaries and projects.

REV. DR. CHRISTOPHER ALAN BULLOCK

Theme: Blow The Trump, Sound The Alarm
Text: Ezekiel 3:1-7

These are perilous, pitiful, and prophetic times. We are living in a decaying, desperate, and decadent world. Just listen to CNN, MSNBC, Fox News, and NPR. Scan the internet, read the NY Times, Washington Post, Chicago Tribune, Philadelphia Inquirer and Tribune, NPR.... it's primarily bad news. Furthermore, we are starving massively in a land of plenty. We have an unparalleled educational crisis in urban schools.

We have brutal oppression in a world of enlightenment. The mood of anxiety is high. There is war and rumors of war instead of peace in the Middle East. There is too much unholy activity in the Holy Land. The blood of our children stains the streets of Philadelphia, Wilmington, and Chester. We must choose the Bible, the Ballot, or the Bullet. Our criminal justice system and prison industrial complex needs repair and reform.

The Black Family unit must be revived, resuscitated, and reformed in the name of help, healing, and hope. We must examine ourselves as a people. The wicked works of black self-destruction have produced the strange fruit of impending doom and gloom. I'm not optimistic and cannot be — in light of the present reality.

Today, at the age of 73, Bro. Chip remains, first and foremost, a preacher of the unsearchable riches of Christ in Kings Mountain and beyond!

Authentic Prophets are not optimistic but bluntly realistic and painfully pessimistic. The piercing question is: *HOW SHALL THE BLACK CHURCH AND PREACHERS RESPOND?* We must *'BLOW THE TRUMPET AND SOUND THE ALARM'* like Ezekiel did in his day. Ezekiel was a tempered temple priest and a major prophet with a major message. God called and commissioned Ezekiel to pronounce Judah and Jerusalem's downfall with severe judgment. Ezekiel prophesied in the midst of Jewish degeneracy and Babylonian arrogance.

This strong and audacious watchman boldly denounced the idolatry of his own people. He called with fervor on a disobedient nation to repent from their sins and return to a righteous God. Ezekiel's prophecy reminds the preacher that we should preach with prophetic boldness without fear or trembling.

Let's be clear: we have those in our midst who need to hear the trumpet blow and respond to the alarm of the Gospel. And they have some questions for us:

- Is there hope for the hood?
- Has God vacated the ghetto?
- Is there a savior for the suburbs?
- Can darkness and co-exist?
- Can the street corner be transformed into the amen corner?
- Is there good news in bad times
- They have some questions for the Black Church.

- Is the church bold enough to move from the pews to the pavement?
- From the sanctuary to the streets
- Has the Black Church become too sanctimonious and insulting of regular folk?

They have some questions: Have we become bound to rustic and rigid religiosity, to dogmas and doctrine - that we have shut out the free flow of the Holy Spirit from moving us in a new direction? Has the preacher put down the trumpet? Is the alarm dead? Are the doors of the churches closed to the demonized, the disinherited, the disenfranchised, and the destitute?

BLOW THE TRUMPET AND SOUND THE ALARM!!

- The Beggars and Bankers, The Scholars and Scoundrels - The Ph.D., the GED, the no D
- The educated, medicated, and the formerly incarcerated.
- They all need the Glorious Gospel of Jesus Christ.

Get their attention and warn the people. Ezekiel saw a valley of dry bones; I like something about Ezekiel. He didn't retreat from his prophetic assignment. He didn't complain about the awful condition of human and spiritual wreckage in his midst. Instead, he prophesied and preached:

Until the Almighty Wind of God's spirit moved, He preached until those dreary, desolate, and dry bones rattled and shook. He preached until a new life sprung up, and hope was resurrected.

He preached until the undeniable, unmistakable, indisputable power of God showed up. Yes, it's dark now; a new day is dawning. 'There's a bright side somewhere. Don't stop preaching until you find it.

YES, THESE DRY BONES IN OUR CHURCHES AND COMMUNITIES CAN LIVE AGAIN. BLOW THE TRUMPET - SOUND THE ALARM.

YES, THEY CAN LIVE AGAIN THROUGH A SAVING GOSPEL

For Paul said: I'M NOT ASHAMED OF THE GOSPEL OF CHRIST; FOR IT IS (NOT WAS) IT IS THE POWER OF GOD UNTO EVERYONE THAT BELIEVETH.

BLOW THE GOSPEL TRUMPET, SOUND THE ALARM!!
WHY?
"FOR THE WORLD IS HUNGRY FOR THE LIVING BREAD,
LIFT THE SAVIOR UP FOR THEM TO SEE.
TRUST HIM - DO NOT DOUBT THE WORDS THAT HE SAID,
1 WILL DRAW ALL MEN UNTO ME
LIFT HIM UP - LIFT HIM UP,
STILL HE SPEAKS FROM ETERNITY.
AND "IF I, BE LIFTED FROM THE EARTH
I WILL DRAW ALL MEN UNTO ME".[33]

---

[33] Rev. Dr. C. Allan Bullock, Senior Pastor, Canaan Missionary Baptist Church New Castle, Delaware, USA. Since 2004,

Dr. Bullock has served as the inaugural Pastor of Canaan Baptist Church of Delaware. The mission of Canaan is to do Ministry for the Master. Canaan is a vibrant community welcoming people from various backgrounds, including the Caribbean, South America, and Africa.

REV. DAVID BEELEN

> Theme: The Making of a Servant Leader: James, the brother of Christ
>
> Text: James 1:1-4

[1].James, a servant of God and of the Lord Jesus Christ, To the twelve tribes scattered among the nations: Greetings. [2] Consider it pure joy, my brothers, and sisters, whenever you face trials of many kinds, [3] because you know that the testing of your faith produces perseverance. [4] Let perseverance finish its work so that you may be mature and complete, not lacking anything.

Dr. Bullock was the first African American elected New Castle County President. Dr. Bullock has also held positions such as president of the Delaware Black Caucus and National Baptist Convention USA, Inc. board member.

He currently serves as Honorary Commander of the Delaware State Police Delaware Committee, U.S. Global Leadership Coalition, and Delaware Supreme Court Sub-Committee of Diversity, Equity, and Inclusion.

Dr. Bullock earned a Doctor of Ministry degree from the United Theological Seminary, specializing in Black Church Leadership in the Urban Context; a Master of Divinity Degree from the Colgate-Rochester Divinity School/Crozer Seminary, with a concentration in Black Church Theology; and a Bachelor of Social Work in criminal justice from the University of Alaska-Anchorage.

As an author, Dr. Bullock has written two books: "The Social Mission of the Black Church: A Call to Action" and "A Charge to Keep." These works reflect his passion for Social Justice and challenge the Black church to return to its roots. In 2023, Dr. Bullock received a special honor while on a preaching mission in Liberia, West Africa. The Chief of the local Kpelle Tribe gowned him at the Liberian Baptist Convention and bestowed upon him "JUTONU," meaning "ONE WHO RESPONDS."

Dr. Bullock shares his life and Ministry with Rev. Dr. Debbie Ardella Strickling-Bullock. Dr. Debbie serves as the Executive Pastor of Canaan Baptist Church. They are blessed with two sons, Benjamin Ellis Bullock and Daniel Alan Bullock, and three grandchildren. (Christopher Alan Bullock. A Charge To Keep. Union Press Printing. For more information, please visit www.canaanbcde.org).

How is your faith?

If your faith were a tree, and I pulled it up by the roots, would the roots be deep? James is a test of your spiritual health. Let's use his letter as a diagnostic tool. This letter is unique because of its author. James, the brother of Jesus, raised in the same home in Nazareth, grew up with Jesus, saw him through all those silent years of which we have no record, and later …joined with his three other brothers-Joseph, Simon, and Judas in opposition to Jesus.

James was converted after Jesus died; Paul tells us that the Lord appeared to James after the resurrection. Imagine that meeting between an older and younger brother. James had deep doubts that Jesus was the Son of God, as he claimed. As he watched Jesus grow up and become a Rabbi, James regarded him as a madman and came with his Mother and brothers to have him committed---or at least go home with them to get Jesus out of the public view.

But finally, by experiencing the resurrection, he was convinced that there indeed was God in the flesh. So, he begins his letter with *James, a servant of God and of the Lord Jesus Christ.* This one, his half-brother by nature, would call him: *"Our Lord Jesus Christ."* Arresting, isn't it? And throughout this letter, you hear a reverence, a kind of affectionate respect for the person of his half-brother.

In the days after the resurrection, James became the leader of the church in Jerusalem and was regarded with honor by all, even by the Jews. He soon had the title "James the Just." Historians tell us that James was finally martyred for his faith by being pushed off the pinnacle of the temple. The pinnacle was the point in the wall around the temple that jutted out over the Kidron Valley. There was a drop of about a hundred feet straight down from the height of that wall. This past summer, I stood there, the very place where I took Jesus and tempted him to jump off.

Historian Eusebius tells us that in the year 62 A.D., James the Just, the brother of our Lord, was pushed off this pinnacle by his enemies who had become angry with him for his Christian testimony. Eusebius says that the fall didn't kill him immediately he managed to crawl up to his knees to pray for his murderers. So, they finished the job by throwing stones at his head till he fell unconscious. He joined the band of martyrs. This man lived and died trusting. Remember the theme of this letter? Faith! James, the former doubter, goes to work building faith and trust.

In chapter one, you have an answer to the question, "What makes faith grow?" Jesus said that it does not take much faith to get going; if you have faith like a grain of mustard seed, just a little bit of it, even though you are filled with doubts, that is enough.

Here is what, James tells us, makes faith grow. Trials. Come to think of it, this is experientially true, isn't it? A whole lot of our songs tell this truth, like this one from Andre Crouch:

Through it all
I thank God for the mountains,
and I thank Him for the valleys,

151

I thank Him for the storms He brought me through.

For if I'd never had a problem,

I wouldn't know God could solve them,

I'd never know what faith in God could do

Through it all, through it all,

I've learned to trust in Jesus,

I've learned to trust in God.

Back to our text, James says...

> [2] Consider it pure joy, my brothers and sisters, whenever you face trials of many kinds, [3] because you know that the testing of your faith produces perseverance.

You need trials. Trees often have root systems that grow deep under one condition: wind. In the early 1980s, there was an experiment called the biodome in the desert. It was an exercise to create the perfect living environment for humans, plants, and animals.

A huge glass dome was constructed, and an artificially controlled environment was created with perfect growing conditions. People lived in the biodome for months at a time, and it was wonderful. Everything seemed to do well except. When the trees grew to be a certain height, they would simply topple over. It baffled scientists 'til they realized the one natural element they forgot to recreate in the biodome: wind! Trees need wind to blow against them, which causes their root systems to grow deeper, supporting the tree as it grows taller.

You don't get mature, tested trees without wind. So also, you don't get mature, tested Christians without trials, says James. He then goes on to describe how to work with trials. Accept them, he says, as from God. Trials produce perseverance, which produces maturity **so that you may be mature and complete.**

The Greek word telos, translated as 'mature,' means that a sacrificial animal was fit to be offered to God. When used to describe a person, it means to be grown up.

That you might be mature then means that you might be fit to be offered as a sacrifice to God and be mature and grown up. It is patience that marks us as mature. How does God develop patience in us? You don't become patient by trying to be patient. We don't just receive it as a gift of the Holy Spirit. It is something that God has chosen to develop in us through trials.

We don't like to hear that; we would rather have instant patience.

"Lord, give me patience…. and I want it right now." We avoid trails. One of the most unpleasant times in school was the days when we had to take a test.

The purpose of the test is to determine how much you have learned. God often puts us through tests to help us discover how much we have learned. It is not for Him to find out; He already knows.

Sometimes, we think that we are further advanced than we really are.

We start to get a little big-headed. So, he puts us to the test to show us the truth about our progress. I hate it when I fail a test; you

153

will have to take it over until you pass. Listen to C S Lewis: A silly idea is current that good people do not know what temptation means. This is a blatant lie. Only those who try to resist temptation know how strong it is. After all, you find out the strength of the German army by fighting against it, not by giving in. You find out the strength of the wind by trying to walk against it, not by lying down. A man who gives in to temptation after five minutes simply does not know what it would have been like an hour later. That is why bad people, in one sense, know very little about badness — they have lived a sheltered life by always giving in. We never find out the strength of the evil impulse inside us until we try to fight it: and Christ, who never yielded to temptation, is also the only man who knows to the full what temptation means — the only complete realist."

Jesus knows trials and temptations, so he is such a great husband. Jesus is our King; yes, he rules. Jesus is our Father; yes, he loves. Jesus is also our husband and teaches us how to be husbands and wives.

I want to share part of a post by Ann Voskamp that humbled me as a husband and made me think of Jesus. If you are single, remember that God blesses singleness. If you are married—especially men—listen carefully.

I have been thinking about perseverance this past week, and it's not *Boring. Can I tell you something, sons? Romance isn't measured by how viral your proposal goes.* The internet age may try to sell you something different, but don't forget that being viral is closely associated with sickness, so don't make being viral your goal.

Your goal is always to make your Christ-focus contagious—*to just one person. It's more than just imagining some romantic proposal.* It's a man who imagines washing puked-on sheets at 2:30 a.m. and plunging out a plugged toilet for the third time this week—*that's true romance.*

The man who imagines slipping his arm around his wife's soft, thickening middle-aged waistline and whispering that he couldn't love her more. Who imagines the manliness of standing bold and unashamed in the express checkout line with only maxi pads and tampons because someone he loves is having an unexpected Saturday morning emergency?

The real romantics imagine greying, sagging, and wrinkling as the deepening of something sacred. *Because get this, kids* — How a man *proposes* isn't what makes him romantic. It's how a man *purposes50* to lay down his *life* that makes him romantic. And a man begins being romantic years before any ring – romance begins with only having eyes for one woman now – so you don't go giving your eyes away to cheap porn.

Your dad will sometimes say it to me as he leans over: "*I am glad that there's always only been you.*" The real romantics know that stretchmarks are beauty marks, that different-shaped women fit into the different shapes of men's souls, and that real romance is really *sacrifice.*

I know – you're thinking, "*Boring.*" *My sons, Don't ever forget:* The real romantics *are* the boring ones— they let another heart *bore a hole deep into theirs. Be one of the boring ones.* Pray to get boring years of marriage *–fifty years to let her heart bore a hole deep into yours.*

Let everyone do their talking about fifty shades of grey, but don't let anyone talk you out of it: commitment is pretty much black and white. Because the truth is, real love will always make you suffer. Simply commit: *For whom am I willing to suffer?* Who am I willing to take the reeking garbage out for and clean out the gross muck ponding at the bottom of the fridge? Who am I willing to listen *to* instead of talk to? Who am I willing to hold as they grow older and more real? Who am I willing to *die* a bit more for every day? Who am I willing to make *heart-boring* years with? *Who am I willing to let bore a hole into my heart?* Get it: Life – and marriage proposals — isn't about *one ups-Manship but one downs-Manship.*

It's about the heart-boring years of sacrifice and going lower and *serving.* It's not about how well you perform your proposal. It's about how well you let Christ transform your life. I'm praying, boys — *be Men.* Be one of the *'boring" men – and let your heart be bored into.* And now there are women who love that kind of man. The type of man whose romance isn't flashy – because love is gritty.

The kind of man whose romance isn't about cameras — because it's about Christ. The type of man whose romance doesn't have to go viral — *because it's going eternal.* No, your dad did not get down on one knee when he proposed – *because romantic men know it's about living your whole life on your knees.* This is beautifully boring; the way two lives touch and go deeper into time, the clock ticking passionately into decades and persevering to the end. Let perseverance finish its work so that you may be mature and complete, not lacking anything.[34]

REV. PAUL L. ANDERSON

> Theme: The True Power of Visionary Leadership
> Text: St. Luke 24:13-34 NLT - The Walk to Emmaus

[13] That same day, two of Jesus' followers were walking to the village of Emmaus, seven miles[a] from Jerusalem. [14] As they walked along, they were talking about everything that had happened. [15] As they talked and discussed these things, Jesus himself suddenly came and began walking with them. [16] But

---

[34] Rev. David Beelen is a visiting instructor at Calvin Theological Seminary in Grand Rapids, Michigan, United States of America.

Rev. David H. Beelen (affectionately called Pastor Dave) joyfully serves together as co-pastor at Madison Square Christian Reformed Church in Grand Rapids, Michigan, North America, with Rev. Dr. Samuel B. Reeves, Jr. (affectionately called Pastor Sam). David is a follower of Jesus, husband to Melanie, Father to three children, and grandfather to two delightful grandsons. He is also a retired Minister of Word and Sacrament in the Christian Reformed Church in North America, living in Grand Rapids, MI. David received his Master of Divinity from Western Calvin Seminary in Grand Rapids, MI 1982.

During his 38 years of pastoral Ministry, David served as lead Pastor at Madison Church in Grand Rapids, a multi-site, multi-ethnic church. In addition, David has served, since 2012, as a visiting instructor at Calvin Seminary and works in the seminary's Vocation Formation Ministry as a Formation Specialist. David has a heart and passion for developing leaders and coaching and encouraging other pastors. His life verse is 2 Timothy 2:2, which says, "And the things you have heard me say in the presence of many witnesses entrust to dependable people who will also be qualified to teach others."

God kept them from recognizing him. [17] He asked them, "What are you discussing so intently as you walk along?" They stopped short, sadness written across their faces. [18] Then one of them, Cleopas, replied, "You must be the only person in Jerusalem who hasn't heard about all the things that have happened there the last few days." [19] "What things?" Jesus asked. "The things that happened to Jesus, the man from Nazareth," they said. "He was a prophet who did powerful miracles, and he was a mighty teacher in the eyes of God and all the people. [20] But our leading priests and other religious leaders handed him over to be condemned to death, and they crucified him. [21] We had hoped he was the Messiah who had come to rescue Israel. This all happened three days ago. [22] "Then some women from our group of his followers were at his tomb early this morning, and they came back with an amazing report. [23] They said his body was missing, and they had seen angels who told them Jesus was alive! [24] Some of our men ran out to see, and sure enough, his body was gone, just as the women had said." [25] Then Jesus said to them, "You foolish people! You find it hard to believe all the prophets wrote in the Scriptures. [26] Wasn't it predicted that the Messiah would suffer all these things before entering his glory?" [27] Then Jesus took them through the writings of Moses and all the prophets, explaining from all the Scriptures the things concerning himself. [28] By this time, they were nearing Emmaus and the end of their journey. Jesus acted as if he were going on [29,] but they begged him, "Stay the night with us since it is getting late." So, he went home with them. [30] As they sat down to eat,[b] he took the bread and blessed it. Then he broke it and gave it to them. [31] Suddenly, their eyes were opened, and they recognized him. And at that moment, he disappeared! [32] They said to each other, "Didn't our hearts burn within us as he talked with us on the road and explained the Scriptures to us?" [33] And within the hour, they were on their way back to Jerusalem. There, they found the eleven disciples and the others who had gathered with them, [34] who said, "The Lord has risen! He appeared to Peter."

In Luke 24:13-34, the narrative of the road to Emmaus unfolds, revealing profound insights into the nature of true leadership. This passage begins with two disciples walking from Jerusalem to Emmaus, reflecting on the recent events of Jesus' crucifixion and the unsettling reports of His resurrection. As we delve into this passage, we uncover essential elements of leadership that are as relevant today as they were in the early church.

Firstly, leadership is about presence. Though unrecognized, the risen Christ comes alongside the disciples on their journey. Walking with them illustrates a fundamental aspect of leadership: the willingness to meet people where they are. Leadership is not about positioning oneself above others but joining them on their journey, especially in moments of confusion and despair. Jesus' presence provided the disciples with a sense of companionship and support, essential for effective leadership.

Secondly, leadership requires listening and understanding. As Jesus walks with the disciples, He asks, *"What are you discussing together as you walk along?" (Luke 24:17).* This question is not rhetorical; it is an invitation for the disciples to share their thoughts and feelings. Great leaders understand the importance of listening. Encouraging open dialogue creates an environment where individuals feel valued and heard. This approach builds trust and fosters a strong relational foundation, crucial for any leadership context.

As the disciples express their disillusionment, Jesus listens patiently. They recount their hope that Jesus was the one to redeem Israel and their confusion over the empty tomb. This interaction highlights another critical aspect of leadership: patience. Effective leaders do not rush to conclusions or solutions; they allow time for reflection and understanding. Jesus' patience in this encounter demonstrates that leaders must be willing to give others the space to voice their concerns and doubts.

After listening to them, Jesus responds not with criticism but with gentle guidance. He explains the Scriptures, starting with Moses and all the Prophets, showing how they point to Himself. This moment is pivotal in the narrative, underscoring the importance of teaching and clarity in leadership. Leaders must have a deep understanding of their mission and be able to communicate it effectively. By illuminating the Scriptures, Jesus provides the disciples with a renewed perspective, transforming their despair into hope.

Moreover, Jesus' approach highlights the significance of leading by example. His knowledge of the Scriptures and His ability to connect them to the current situation inspire confidence and trust in

His leadership. Leaders who demonstrate expertise and insight can effectively guide others through uncertainty and doubt.

Another essential lesson in leadership from this passage is the importance of recognizing and seizing teachable moments. He agrees when the disciples reach Emmaus and invite Jesus to stay with them. At the table, Jesus takes bread, gives thanks, breaks it, and begins to give it to them. In this simple yet profound act, their eyes are opened, and they recognize Him. This moment of revelation underscores that leadership often involves identifying the right moment to impart wisdom or insight. Effective leaders are attuned to these opportunities and use them to foster growth and understanding in others.

Furthermore, breaking bread is a powerful symbol of community and fellowship. Leadership is not just about guiding others but also about fostering a sense of belonging and unity. By breaking bread with the disciples, Jesus reinforces the importance of communal bonds and shared experiences in the leadership journey.

The disciples' immediate reaction upon recognizing Jesus was to return to Jerusalem to share the news. This response illustrates the ripple effect of effective leadership. True leadership inspires others to take action and become leaders themselves. The disciples' transformation from despair to fervent witnesses of the resurrection exemplifies how leadership can empower and mobilize individuals for a greater purpose.

In addition, this passage highlights the transformative power of visionary leadership. Jesus provided the disciples with a vision that transcended their immediate circumstances. By reframing their understanding of the Scriptures and revealing His resurrection, He gave them a new perspective on their mission and purpose. Visionary leaders have the ability to see beyond the present challenges and inspire others with a compelling vision of the future.

Another key aspect of leadership demonstrated in this passage is humility. Despite being the risen Lord, Jesus does not impose Himself on the disciples. He engages with them as a fellow traveler and respects their invitation to stay. This humility is a crucial quality in leadership. It shows that true leaders do not seek to dominate but to serve and uplift others. By embodying humility, leaders create an atmosphere of mutual respect and collaboration.

Moreover, Jesus' interaction with the disciples on the road to Emmaus teaches us about the importance of resilience in leadership. The disciples were disheartened and struggling to understand the events they had witnessed. Jesus' patience and guidance helped them regain their faith and purpose.

Effective leaders help followers navigate difficulties and uncertainties, instilling resilience and perseverance. The story of the Road to Emmaus also emphasizes the importance of continuous learning and growth in leadership. Jesus used the opportunity to expand the disciples' understanding of the Scriptures, demonstrating that leaders should always seek to learn and grow, both personally and collectively, with their followers. This commitment to ongoing education and development is essential for sustaining effective leadership.

Furthermore, this passage highlights the importance of adaptability in leadership. Jesus adapted His approach based on the disciples' needs and emotional state. Effective leaders are flexible and responsive, able to adjust their strategies and methods to support and guide their followers.

In conclusion, the narrative of the road to Emmaus in Luke 24:13-34 provides a rich tapestry of insights into the nature of leadership. It teaches us that leadership is about presence, listening, patience, teaching, leading by example, recognizing teachable moments, fostering community, inspiring action, visionary thinking, humility, resilience, continuous learning, and adaptability. By embodying these qualities, leaders can effectively guide and empower others, fostering a sense of purpose and unity in their journey together. As we reflect on this passage, let us strive to emulate the leadership of Jesus, walking alongside others with compassion, wisdom, and humility and inspiring them to reach their full potential in the service of a greater mission.[35]

---

[35] Reverend Paul L. Anderson is the Pastor of The Fountain of Raleigh Fellowship in Raleigh, North Carolina. Before establishing The Fountain of Raleigh, he served for seventeen and a half years as Pastor of Baptist Grove Church in Raleigh, NC, and previously as Pastor of Rock Spring Baptist Church in Creedmoor, NC.

Pastor Anderson was born and raised in Charlotte, NC, where he accepted his call and became licensed in the Gospel Ministry by the University Park Baptist Church, Charlotte, NC. He earned a Bachelor of Business Administration degree concentrating in Management Science from North Carolina Central University (NCCU) in Durham, NC. He participated in the First Union National Bank of North Carolina Consumer Associate Program upon graduating. First Baptist Church,

Raleigh, NC, later ordained him. He received a Master of Divinity degree with a focus in Christian Education from Southeastern Baptist Theological Seminary in Wake Forest, NC.

Pastor Anderson has been serving his community for many years. He currently serves as the Senior Chaplain volunteer for the City of Raleigh Police Department and the Police Chief's I-C.A.R.E. Team. He also serves on the Boards of Directors for Uplift Project Incorporated, Oak City Outreach, Hebron Colony Ministries, Mechanics and Farmers Bank Raleigh Advisory Board, and the North Carolina State University Chancellor's African American Community Advisory Council. Pastor Anderson has served as Moderator for the Wake Missionary Baptist Association and a member of the Ministerial Board.

As a member of the General Baptist State Convention of NC, Inc., he has served in the following capacities: Chair for the Personnel Committee, Management Team, Evangelism, Prison, and Cooperative Ministry Committees, Dean for the Congress of Christian Education, and Editor for the Baptist Informer. Pastor Anderson is also a Cooperative Baptist Fellowship International member, serving on local and statewide committees. He is also on the Ordaining Council for the Raleigh Baptist Association. He previously served on the City of Raleigh Planning Commission and Pedestrian and Bicycle Commission and was a Leadership Council Member for the Wake County 10-Year Action Plan to End Homelessness.

Pastor Anderson holds Life Memberships in Omega Psi Phi Fraternity, NAACP, and North Carolina Central University Alumni Association. He is also a member of the Sons of the American Revolution, which means he has a "Revolutionary War Patriot Ancestor by the name of Walter Hanson (1760-17920) and is a close relative of President John Hanson (April 13, 1721 - November 22, 1783). John Hanson was the United States' First President in Congress Assembled (THE ORIGINAL UNITED STATES GOVERNMENT) - under the U.S. Articles of Confederation".

Among the many awards and recognitions Pastor Anderson has received for his commitment, dedication, and service to the community are the Citizen of the Year Award (2009) given by Beta Phi Chapter of Omega Psi Fraternity, Inc.; the NCCU Hall of Fame Award (2006); and the John Chavis Community Legacy Award (2019).

Pastor Anderson is married to (Reverend) Tina Morris-Anderson; they have two sons: Paul L. Anderson, II, and Noah J. Anderson. Both of their sons are proud members of Omega Psi Phi Fraternity, Inc., and Phi Mu Alpha Sinfonia (Music) Fraternity, Inc.

REV. LAURA CARPENTER PRITCHARD

Theme: Real Leaders Rest
Text: Exodus 20

8. "Remember the Sabbath day by keeping it holy. 9 Six days you shall labor and do all your work, 10 but the seventh day is a Sabbath to the Lord your God. On it you shall not do any work, neither you, nor your son, nor daughter, nor your male or female servant, nor your animals, nor any foreigner residing in your towns. 11 For in six days the Lord made the heavens and the earth, the sea, and all that is in them, but he rested on the seventh day. Therefore, the Lord blessed the Sabbath day and made it holy.

We often think of *being* unproductive, but that is so wrong and counterproductive. Because we are so accustomed to going and doing, *we still* feel strange, odd, and wrong. If our bodies are not moving, our fingers are moving, and if we put our devices away, our minds are moving, thinking, planning, and devising.

You were just thinking that this week, as soon as I finish this project, I am going to take a few days off …, and then the next project comes.

Real Leaders must produce. Real Leaders must show tangible results.

Real Leaders have to keep everyone else going. Yes, these things are true, but here is something leaders often neglect and/or forget.

Real Leaders Rest!

165

While reading Gordan MacDonald's book, Ordering Your Private World, I learned how important Sabbath keeping was to William Wilberforce, the Christian leader, and politician who served in the British Parliament and was the leading voice in convincing the British Parliament to end slavery in the British Empire. Wilberforce was very ambitious and passionate about his political work. According to Garth Lean, one of Wilberforce's biographers, "By his admissions, he had 'risings of ambition,' and it was crippling his soul." For Wilberforce, keeping the Sabbath was vital to his life rhythm; Garth Lean also said, "Sunday brought the cure."

Wilberforce rested weekly from all of his vocational strivings. In his journal, he wrote, "Blessed be to God for the day of rest, and religious occupation wherein earthly things assume their true size. Ambition is stunted."

Sabbath brought perspective to Wilberforce's life. It seems that he was able to realign his intentions with God's purposes. Wilberforce knew the value of the Sabbath and lived a Sabbath-keeping life. Wilberforce was a Real Leader who knew how to Rest!

The Hebrew translation of the Sabbath is cease, desist, rest. To Sabbath is to stop. To be clear, the Sabbath is to rest. You can Sabbath when you know it is not all about you. In Sabbath keeping, we acknowledge our limits and God's limitlessness. God is the one doing whatever must be done; we are his dispensable instruments. Wow! That is humbling; we are dispensable. Are we God's handiwork, created to do the good works he has prepared for us to do? Yes! But he is the creator, not us. In Sabbath keeping, we acknowledge that it is not all about us.

Consider this acronym when you think about Sabbath–

R - Rhythm

E - Experience

S - Submission

T - Training

Rhythm

According to author Pete Scazzero's book Emotionally Healthy Spirituality, "Sabbath is engaging in a regular rhythm of stopping, resting, delighting, and contemplating God for a 24-hour block of time each week."

> Exodus 20:10 says the seventh day is a sabbath to the Lord, your God. Every seventh day, we are to cease, desist, and rest to the Lord our God. The Lord himself rested on the seventh day. He commands us to set it apart and give it to him. The rhythm is every week.

Experience

The Sabbath is designed for us to experience the Lord. To commune with God. To connect with God and, in so doing, for Him to communicate with us. We often get lost in all the doing and going.

Jesus said in Matthew 11, 28 "Come to me, all you who are weary and burdened, and I will give you rest. 29 Take my yoke upon you and learn from me, for I am gentle and humble in heart, and you will find rest for your souls. 30 For my yoke is easy, and my burden is light."

According to Mark 2:27, the Sabbath was made for us not to be burdened by legal restrictions, but to have proper rest. As the Matthew text says, for us to learn from God, who is God. For us to find rest for our (weary) souls.

I know you need rest for your soul! Real Leaders Rest.

Submission

Sabbath is an act of submission to God's will and way, to his command, to do as God did. So, I follow God in my lifestyle, submitting all that I am and all my responsibilities to Him, trusting his plan, purpose, and power.

Hebrews 4

> "Today, if you hear his voice, do not harden your hearts." 8 For if Joshua had given them rest, God would not have spoken later about another day. 9 There remains, then, a Sabbath-rest for the people of God; ten for anyone who enters God's rest also rests from their [works, [e] just as God did from his.

Submit and enter the Sabbath rest.

Real Leaders Rest

Training

Sabbath requires commitment and intention, just like training. Sabbath does not just happen. We must train ourselves to rest rhythmically, be still, know God, and submit to God. And if we do, we will find, like William Wilberforce, that Sabbath brings the cure.

Yes! Work with all your heart as unto the Lord, the 6 days that our God has given you. And on the seventh day, receive the gift of Sabbath, your rest, and your ceasing. The Sabbath is made for you! Enjoy God! Enjoy yourself in the Lord. And I know just like Jesus healed the sick on the Sabbath, you will find your healing as you find your rest in the Lord.

> Isaiah 30 says–15 This is what the Sovereign Lord, the Holy One of Israel, says: "In repentance and rest is your salvation, in quietness and trust is your strength, but you would have none of it."

I could hardly write this sermon! Maybe you, like me, need to repent and rest. We need to quiet ourselves and trust. That is where we will find our strength. Let us pray together, "Lord, I repent of my busyness and neglect of the Sabbath that you offer me. Lord, help me regularly—Sabbath in you—still, my heart and mind. Help me to trust that all I need to do will get done. Help me to trust your healing power to work in me as I Sabbath. Show me what the true Sabbath is and help me live it out in my life. I entrust everything to you. In Jesus' name, Amen."

Howard Thurman said, "It is good to make an end of movement, to come to a point of rest, a place of pause. There is some strange magic in activity, in keeping at it, in continuing to be involved in many things that excite the mind and keep the hours swiftly passing. But it is a deadly magic; one is not wise to trust it with too much confidence."

Remember, Leader, Real Leaders Rest![36]

---

[36] Rev. Laura Carpenter Pritchard Director, Sister, Church Relations Providence Baptist Church Monrovia, Liberia

After more than 25 years of full-time Ministry in Michigan at Madison Square Church, Rev. Laura Pritchard is now serving as a missionary for the Christian Reformed Church of North America (CRCNA) in Liberia, West Africa. She is working to fulfill her dream, which started with a prayer in 2005. She asked the Lord to make her an agent of healing and restoration, a bridge between African Americans and Africans. Her primary missional focus is to be an agent of healing, reconciliation, and empowerment. Working to build constructive connections between African Americans and West Africans, starting in Liberia.

Laura worked with Rev. Dr. Samuel B. Reeves from 1997 to 2005 when he served as co-pastor at Madison Square Church, and Laura was Director of Youth Ministry. Under the leadership of Rev. Reeves, Laura's first trip to Liberia in 2001 and her next trip in 2005 were life-changing, setting her on the trajectory of living, serving, and loving Liberia.

Laura says she is home. She lives in Liberia with her husband, Henry Pritchard, and their daughter, Thelma. She was ordained as Minister of the Word in 2019. She is the Director of Sister Church Relations at the historic Providence Baptist Church, once again serving with Rev. Reeves.

Laura preaches, teaches, and invests in leadership development with emerging leaders at Providence Baptist Church.

[Many West African countries have a "Door of No Return," but Liberia is our "Door of Return!" I long for my brothers and sisters from the States to come *home*. To come and learn, to connect. I pray for us to learn our common history. To eat Collard greens together. To sing together. To pray together. To work together. To grow together. To heal together.]

CONCLUSION

As I did in the first book of this series, I'd like to thank you again for taking us on this wonderful journey through the second book of the Surveying the Leadership Landscape series.

In this sequel of the Leadership Landscape series, we have argued again that leaders are not just like everyone else. Why? I am glad you asked. Because leaders are not. They see and imagine the world differently than those around them. Leaders are on top, out front, and ahead of the pack. They are watchmen looking over the horizon, identifying challenges from a distance, and inspiring those they lead on the journey to accomplish what God has called them to.

Together, in this book, we have learned, in essence, that is exactly what a leader does. We have had the opportunity to study and learn from one of the greatest leaders of all time. We watched and walked alongside Nehemiah as he guided his team to a great victory. He taught us the importance of being a three hundred and sixty degrees (360°) leader, the ability to lead oneself (leading self), the ability to lead your superior - those who are in charge (leading up), the ability to lead your

171

peer; and equals (leading laterally); and the ability to lead those who are accountable to you (leading down).

As leaders, we have learned from Nehemiah, as shared in this book, that victory is never ours. It is always of God, from God, and for God. He is the Ultimate Leader, and He calls leaders like you and me to be on His team and to ride the waves He has created for us.

We studied seven essential characteristics of leadership: caring for the work you are called to do; knowing where your help comes from - praying for help; the ability to lead other leaders; motivating followers; organizing the work, to handle the opposition, and finally, the leader's ability to leave the place they had served, better than they encountered it. We learned the importance of choosing the right leaders in business, education, medicine, or other areas of life, be it at home, in the community, in the Church, or in the state. When these characteristics are practiced, the leader, like Nehemiah, becomes a competent leader and a master influencer.

Nehemiah, the central figure of this series, led the third of three expeditions by the Jewish people following their seventy years of exile in Babylon. He described how he rebuilt Jerusalem during the Second Temple period. Under Nehemiah's leadership, the Jews withstood opposition and came together to accomplish their goal. Nehemiah led by example, giving up a respected position in a palace for hard labor in a politically insignificant district.

He teaches us how to partner with others to solidify the political and spiritual foundations of the people God calls us to lead. His humility before God, as seen in his intercessory prayers in chapters 1 and 9, provides an example. He teaches us not to claim glory for ourselves but to always give God credit for our blessings and successes.

Nehemiah's study shows us the significant impact a leader can have and should have on a nation. Nehemiah served in secular offices, using his position to bring back order to the Jews, stability, and proper focus on God. God uses all manner of people in all manner of places, doing all manner of work, to accomplish all manner of results. Leaders must always realize that God has placed them where they are for a purpose. In the word of Rick Warren, leaders are called by God to be purpose-driven. Leaders must have this attitude about their work: "Whatever you do in word or deed, do all in the name of the Lord Jesus, giving thanks through Him to God the Father" (Colossians 3:17).

Nehemiah was a man of prayer, and he prayed passionately for his people (Nehemiah 1). His zealous intercession for God's people foreshadowed our great Intercessor, Jesus Christ, who prayed fervently for His people in His high-priestly prayer in John 17. Both Nehemiah and Jesus had a burning love for God's people, which they poured out in prayer to God, interceding for the people they led before the throne.

Nehemiah led the Israelites to respect and love the Scripture because of his love for God and desire to see God honored and glorified. He led the Israelites towards the faith and obedience God had desired for them for so many years. In the same way, today's leaders must love and revere the truths of Scripture; they must commit them to memory ("Thy Word have I hid in my heart that I may not sin against Thee") as they meditate on them day and night; and turn to them to fulfill every spiritual need, and help them lead well. Secondly, Timothy 3:16–17 tells us, "All scripture is given by inspiration of God, and is profitable for doctrine, reproof, correction, instruction in righteousness: that the man of God may be perfect, thoroughly furnished unto all good works." If we expect to experience the spiritual revival of the Israelites (Nehemiah 8:1-8), we must begin with God's Word.

In our search for competent leadership, we need leaders who have genuine compassion for others, especially those they will lead who have spiritual or physical hurts. To feel compassion yet do nothing to help is unfounded biblically. At times, leaders may have to give up their comfort to minister properly to others. Leaders must believe in a cause before giving their time or money to it with the right heart.

Even unbelievers will know it is God's work when we allow God to minister through exemplary leadership. The pattern is clear throughout history. Whether it was on Nehemiah's day, whether it's in our day, or whether it's in the future, we all fall into one of two categories. You are either with the group exalting the hero or with the rebellious group in the enemy's camp. Either way, you will be exposed. There is no way to cover up to whom you belong.

Jesus said that a tree is known by its fruit.

The fruit is evidence now and will be judged later. And when it is judged, you will hear one of two things. Either you will hear, "Well done, good and faithful servant. Thou hast been faithful over a few things; I will make thee ruler over many things. Enter thou into the joy of thy Lord." That's what I want to hear. But not all of us will hear that. Because many will hear the terrifying words of Matthew 7:23: "I never knew you: depart from me, ye that work iniquity." Do you know which one you're going to hear?

SOURCES

D. Martyn Lloyd-Jones. Preaching & Preachers. Zondervan Publishing House. Grand Rapids, Michigan. 1971.

James Montgomery Boice. Nehemiah: Learning to Lead. Old Tappen: Fleming H. Revell Company, 1990.

J. Oswald Sanders. Spiritual Leadership, Moody Publishers. 2017.

Hans Finzel. The Top Ten Mistakes Leaders Make. Colorado Springs: David C. Cook, 2007.

Chuck Swindoll. Hand Me Another Brick. Word Publishing. Nashville, Tennessee. 1978.

John Maxwell. 21 Irrefutable Laws of Leadership. Harper Collins. Nashville, Tennessee 1998.

John Maxwell. The Maxwell Leadership Bible. Thomas Nelson Publishers. Nashville, Tennessee. 2002.

John MacArthur, The Book on Leadership. Thomas Nelson. Nashville, Tennessee. 2004.

The names of all 20 Presidential Candidates in the Liberian Election: Boakai, Joseph N.: Unity Party (UP), Weah, George Manneh:

Coalition for Democratic Change (CDC), Appleton, Jr. Edward W: Grass Root Democratic Movement (GDM), Kamara, Sr, Lusinee F: All Liberia Coalition Party (ALCOP), Cummings, Alexander B.: Collaborating Political Parties (CPP), Gongloe, Tiawan Saye: Liberia People Party (LPP), Brown, Jr. Allen R: Liberia Restoration Party (LRP), Freeman, Simeon C.M: Movement for Progressive Change (MPC), Tuider, William Wiah: Democrat National Alliance (DNA), Turner, Joshua Tom: New Liberia Party (NLP), Whapoe, Jeremiah Z.: Vision for Liberia Transformation (VOLT), Yorfee, Luther N.: (REBUILDERS), Kromah, Bendu Alehma: Independent (IND), Moniba, Clarence K.: Liberia National Union (LINU), Kouyateh, Sherikh A.: Liberia First Movement (LFM), Kiamu , David GB: Democratic People's Party of Liberia (DPPL), Kollie, Alexander N.: Reformer National Congress (RNC), Nyanti, Sara Beysolow: African Liberation League (ALL), Morris, Robert Franz: Independent (IND), and Miller, Richard Saye: Liberian for Prosperity Party (LFP).

Ron Ashkenas & Brook Manville. Harvard Business Review: Leader's Handbook.

Bill Hybels, Courageous Leadership: Field-Tested Strategy for the 360 Leader, Zondervan: Grand Rapids, MI 2003.

Peter Drucker, Effective Executive. Harper Collins. Nashville, Tennessee. 2006.

Michael Useen. Leading Up. How to Lead Your Boss So You Both Win. p.13

John Maxwell. The 360 Degree Leader Workbook. Thomas Nelson, Nashville, Tennessee. 2006.

John Maxwell. The 360-Degree Leaders: Developing Your Influence from Anywhere in the Organization. Thomas Nelson Press. Nashville, Tennessee. 2005.

Wokie Weah. Proverbs for Beginner: Wisdom Teaching to Set Your Soul on Fire. President Emeritus, Youthpraise. Minneapolis, Minnesota 2021.

William BGK Harris. Liberia's Cultural Great Treasuries: Celebrating Our Cultural Heritage. Improved Solution.com Queetaco Enterprises LCC Atlanta, Georgia 2021.

Samuel B. Reeves, Jr. Surveying the Leadership Landscape: Indispensable Qualities of Leadership. www.improvedsolutions.com: 2020.

Charles R. Swindoll. Hand Me Another Brick: Timeless Lessons on Leadership. Thomas Nelson, xi, 1998

Nehemiah and the Dynamics of Effective Leadership.

President Ellen Johnson-Sirleaf served as the first female democratically elected president and head of state in Liberia and on the continent of Africa. She was the 2011 Nobel Peace Prize winner. Sirleaf was awarded the Nobel Peace Prize for her non-violent efforts to promote peace and her struggle for women's rights. She served as President of the Republic of Liberia from 2005 to 2016. He created peace and economic progress in Liberia and strengthened women's rights. President Sirleaf expanded freedom of speech and became an example for other African and world leaders. Internationally known as Africa's "Iron Lady," Ellen, after serving as President of Liberia, is a leading promoter of peace, justice, and democratic rule.

President George Mannah Weah served as President of the Republic of Liberia from 2017 to 2023. President Weah represented Liberia at the international level, winning 75 caps, scoring 18 goals for his country, and playing at the African Cup of Nations on two occasions. Widely regarded as one of the greatest African players ever, he was named FIFA World Player of the Year and won the Ballon d'Or. He became the first and only player to win these awards while representing an African country internationally. In 1989 and 1995, President Weah was also named the African Footballer of the Year, winning the official award twice. In 1996, he was named African Player of the Century. He is known for his acceleration, speed, and dribbling ability, in addition to his goalscoring and finishing; he was described by FIFA as "the precursor of the multifunctional strikers of today." in 2004, Weah was named by the great Pele in the FIFA 100 list of the world's greatest living players.

A Quick Review of the Approved 2023 National Budget, p. 2. The national budget outlines how much money the government plans to generate and spend in a fiscal year. According to Section 65(1) of the Amendment and Restatement of the amended PFM Act of 2021, the Government of Liberia, through the Ministry of Finance and Development Planning, estimated an amount of US$782.94 million for the national budget for FY2O23, which marks the Second Beginning of a New Fiscal Period (January 1–December 31). The government anticipates overall revenue of US782.94 million this year, with an anticipated US672.94 million coming from domestic sources and US110 million coming from external resources. However, little to no funds were allotted to finance projects in the social sectors (Education and Health), and agriculture received no budget, implying that no large capital projects for these sectors were intended to be implemented in this fiscal year.

John C. Maxwell, The Maxwell Leadership Bible: Lessons in Leadership from the Word of God.

Bill Hybels, Courageous Leadership. Zondervan. Grand Rapids, Michigan. 2002.

Ken Blanchard. Leading At A Higher Level. FT Press May 14, 2023.

Henry and Richard Blackaby, Spiritual Leadership, pages 149-150).

Bill Hybels, Courageous Leadership. Zondervan, Grand Rapids, MI.,

Charles R. Swindoll, Hand Me Another Brick. Work Publishing Nashville, Tennessee, Thomas Nelson.1978.

Michael Useem, Leading Up. How To Lead Your Boss So You Both Sin. Radom House. New York, New York. 2001.

How To Win Friends and Influence People. New York: Simon & Schuster, 1963,

The New Interpreter's Bible Commentary Vol.??? pp. 55-56.

Daniel Goldman. What Makes A Leader. HOR's 10 Must Read. On Emotional Intelligence. Harvard Business Review Press. Boston Massachusetts. 2015. p. 14.

John Maxwell. The 360 Degree Leader Workbook. Thomas Nelson, Nashville, Tennessee. 2006. pp. 206-207.

Jefferson to the New Haven Merchants, July 12, 1801, in PTJ, 34:554. Press copy available online from the Library of Congress. Transcription is available at Founders Online. The source of the above-mentioned paraphrase, which has been mistaken for a direct quote, is John B. McMaster's History of the People of the United

States, which describes Jefferson's statement as follows: "Jefferson's reply to the remonstrance was a discussion of the tenure of office and soon forgotten. But one sentence will undoubtedly be remembered till our Republic ceases to exist. No turn, the Executive ceases to exist. No duty the Executive had to perform was so trying he observed as to put the right man in the right place" John Bach McMaster. History of the People of the United States (New York: Appleton, 1921). 2:586.

The New Interpreter's Bible Commentary. Vol. III. Abingdon Press. pp. 770-771.

Ron Ashkenas & Brook Manville. Harvard Business Review Leader's Handbook: Make An Impact, Inspire Your Organization, and Get to the Next Level. Harvard Business Review Press. Boston, Massachusetts. In chapter 3 of this book, Thomas J. Watson, Jr. is quoted as saying: "I believe the real difference between success and failure in a corporation can be very often traced to how well the organization brings out the great energies and talents of its people".

Junior Freeman and African Soldier are Liberian Artists who wrote the famous Liberian song: THAT MY AREA.

John Maxwell. The 360-Degree Leaders: Developing Your Influence From Anywhere in the Organization. Thomas Nelson Press. Nashville, Tennessee. 2005. pp.159-160.

Christopher Alan Bullock. A Charge To Keep. Union Press Printing.

Karkay Adrienne Tingba 10 Popular Liberian Adages and their Meanings. Koloqua Dialogues, Preserving the Liberian Story in Wetin Happen. May 2, 2019

Lulu V. Marshall, A Book of Liberian Parables: Wise Sayings and their Simple Interpretations. Archway Publishing, Bloomington: Indiana. 2015.

Sid Buzzell, General Editor. The Leadership Bible (NIV): Leadership Principles From God's Word. Zondervan Publishing House: Grand Rapids, Michigan

D. Martyn Lloyd-Jones. Preaching & Preachers. Zondervan Publishing House. Grand Rapids, Michigan. 1971. pages 110 - 111.

James Montgomery Boice. Nehemiah: Learning to Lead. Old Tappen: Fleming H. Revell Company, 1990, page 16.

Martin Lloyd-Jones (Preaching & Preachers. pages 110-111).

J. Oswald Sanders. Spiritual Leadership, Moody Publishers. 2017. p.21.

Hans Finzel. The Top Ten Mistakes Leaders Make. Colorado Springs: David C. Cook, 2007, page 19.

Chuck Swindoll. Hand Me Another Brick. Word Publishing. Nashville, Tennessee. 1978. page 16.

John Maxwell. 21 Irrefutable Laws of Leadership. Harper Collins. Nashville, Tennessee 1998

John Maxwell. The Maxwell Leadership Bible. Thomas Nelson Publishers. Nashville, Tennessee. 2002. p. 779.

John MacArthur, The Book on Leadership. Thomas Nelson. Nashville, Tennessee. 2004. page v.

The names of all 20 Presidential Candidates in the Liberian Election: BOAKAI, JOSEPH N.: Unity Party (UP), WEAH, GEORGE MANNEH: Coalition for Democratic Change (CDC), APPLETON, JR, EDWARD W: Grass Root Democratic Movement (GDM), KAMARA, SR, LUSINEE F: All Liberia Coalition Party (ALCOP), CUMMINGS, ALEXANDER B.: Collaborating Political Parties (CPP), GONGLOE, TIAWAN SAYE: Liberia People Party (LPP), BROWN, JR, ALLEN R: Liberia Restoration Party (LRP), FREEMAN, SIMEON C.M: Movement for Progressive Change (MPC), TUIDER, WILLIAM WIAH: Democrat National Alliance (DNA), TURNER, JOSHUA TOM: New Liberia Party (NLP), WHAPOE, JEREMIAH Z.: Vision for Liberia Transformation (VOLT), YORFEE, LUTHER N.: (REBUILDERS), KROMAH, BENDU ALEHMA: INDEPENDENT (IND), MONIBA, CLARENCE K.: Liberia National Union (LINU), KOUYATEH, SHERIKH A.: Liberia First Movement (LFM), KIAMU, DAVID GB: Democratic People's Party of Liberia (DPPL), KOLLIE, ALEXANDER N.: Reformer National Congress (RNC), NYANTI, SARA BEYSOLOW: African Liberation League (ALL), MORRIS, ROBERT FRANZ: Independent (IND), and MILLER, RICHARD SAYE: Liberian for Prosperity Party (LFP).

Ron Ashkenas & Brook Manville. Harvard Business Review: Leader's Handbook. pp. 4-6.

Bill Hybels, Courageous Leadership: Field-Tested Strategy for the 360 Leader, Zondervan: Grand Rapids, MI 2003, p. 181.

Peter Drucker, Effective Executive. Harper Collins. Nashville, Tennessee. 2006. p.???

Michael Useen. Leading Up. How to Lead Your Boss So You Both Win. p.13

John Maxwell. The 360 Degree Leader Workbook. Thomas Nelson, Nashville, Tennessee. 2006. pages 201-201

John Maxwell. The 360-Degree Leaders: Developing Your Influence from Anywhere in the Organization. Thomas Nelson Press. Nashville, Tennessee. 2005. pp.159-160.

Wokie Weah. Proverbs for Beginner: Wisdom Teaching to Set Your Soul on Fire. President Emeritus, Youth Praise. Minneapolis, Minnesota 2021.

William BGK Harris. Liberia's Cultural Great Treasuries: Celebrating Our Cultural Heritage. Improved Solution.com Queetaco Enterprises LCC Atlanta, Georgia 2021. pp. 8-9.

Samuel B. Reeves, Jr. Surveying the Leadership Landscape: Indispensable Qualities of Leadership. www.improved2life.com: 2020. p.11.

Charles R. Swindoll. Hand Me Another Brick: Timeless Lessons on Leadership. Thomas Nelson, xi, 1998

Nehemiah and the Dynamics of Effective Leadership, page 14.

President Ellen Johnson-Sirleaf served as the first female democratically elected president and head of state in Liberia and on the continent of Africa. She was the 2011 Nobel Peace Prize winner. Sirleaf was awarded the Nobel Peace Prize for her non-violent efforts to promote peace and her struggle for women's rights. She served as President of the Republic of Liberia from 2005 to 2016. He created peace and economic progress in Liberia and strengthened women's rights. President Sirleaf expanded freedom of speech and became an example for other African and world leaders. Internationally known as

Africa's "Iron Lady," Ellen, after serving as President of Liberia, is a leading promoter of peace, justice, and democratic rule.

President George Mannah Weah served as President of the Republic of Liberia from 2017 to 2023. President Weah represented Liberia at the international level, winning 75 caps, scoring 18 goals for his country, and playing at the African Cup of Nations on two occasions. Widely regarded as one of the greatest African players ever, he was named FIFA World Player of the Year and won the Ballon d'Or. He became the first and only player to win these awards while representing an African country internationally. In 1989 and 1995, President Weah was also named the African Footballer of the Year, winning the official award twice. In 1996, he was named African Player of the Century. He is known for his acceleration, speed, and dribbling ability, in addition to his goalscoring and finishing; he was described by FIFA as "the precursor of the multifunctional strikers of today." in 2004, Weah was named by the great Pele in the FIFA 100 list of the world's greatest living players.

A quick review of the Approved 2023 National Budget, p. 2. The national budget outlines how much money the government plans to generate and spend in a fiscal year. According to Section 65(1) of the Amendment and Restatement of the amended PFM Act of 2021, the Government of Liberia, through the Ministry of Finance and Development Planning, estimated an amount of US$782.94 million for the national budget for FY2O23, which marks the Second Beginning of a New Fiscal Period (January 1–December 31). The government anticipates overall revenue of US782.94 million this year, with an anticipated US672.94 million coming from domestic sources and US110 million coming from external resources. However, little to no funds were allotted to finance projects in the social sectors (Education and Health), and agriculture received no budget, implying that no large capital projects for these sectors were intended to be implemented in this fiscal year.

John C. Maxwell, The Maxwell Leadership Bible: Lessons in Leadership from the Word of God. p. 575-578.

Bill Hybels, Courageous Leadership. Zondervan. Grand Rapids, Michigan. 2002. pp. 186-197,

Ken Blanchard. Leading At A Higher Level. FT Press May 14, 2023.

John Maxwell

Henry and Richard Blackaby, Spiritual Leadership, pages 149-150).

Bill Hybels, Courageous Leadership. Zondervan, Grand Rapids, MI., p. 181-197.

Michael Useem, Leading Up: How to Lead Your Boss so You Both Win. pp. 7-8

Charles R. Swindoll, Hand Me Another Brick, page 48.

Michael Useen, Leading Up. p.8

How To Win Friends and Influence People. New York: Simon & Schuster, 1963, page 19.

J. Oswald Sanders (Spiritual Leadership, page 67).

The New Interpreter's Bible Commentary Vol.??? pp. 55-56.

Daniel Goldman. What Makes A Leader. HOR's 10 Must Read. On Emotional Intelligence. Harvard Business Review Press. Boston Massachusetts. 2015. p. 14.

John Maxwell. The 360 Degree Leader Workbook. Thomas Nelson, Nashville, Tennessee. 2006. pp. 206-207.

Jefferson to the New Haven Merchants, July 12, 1801, in PTJ, 34:554. Press copy available online from the Library of Congress. Transcription is available at Founders Online. The source of the above-mentioned paraphrase, which has been mistaken for a direct quote, is John B. McMaster's History of the People of the United States, which describes Jefferson's statement as follows: "Jefferson's reply to the remonstrance was a discussion of the tenure of office and soon forgotten. But one sentence will undoubtedly be remembered till our Republic ceases to exist. No tury the Executive ceases to exist. No duty the Executive had to perform was so trying he observed as to put the right man in the right place" John Bach McMaster. History of the People of the United States (New York: Appleton, 1921). 2:586.

John Maxwell. The Maxwell Leadership Bible. New King James version. Thomas Nelson Bibles. pp. 580-581.

The New Interpreter's Bible Commentary. Vol. III. Abingdon Press. pp. 770-771.

Ron Ashkenas & Brook Manville. Harvard Business Review Leader's Handbook: Make An Impact, Inspire Your Organization, and Get to the Next Level. Harvard Business Review Press. Boston, Massachusetts. p.77. In chapter 3 of this book, Thomas J. Watson, Jr. is quoted as saying: "I believe the real difference between success and failure in a corporation can be very often traced to how well the organization brings out the great energies and talents of its people."

Junior Freeman and African Soldier are Liberian Artists who wrote the famous Liberian song: THAT MY AREA.

John Maxwell. The 360-Degree Leaders: Developing Your Influence From Anywhere in the Organization. Thomas Nelson Press. Nashville, Tennessee. 2005. pp.159-160.

Christopher Alan Bullock. A Charge To Keep. Union Press Printing. For more information, please visit www.canaanbcde.org

Kenneth W. Osbeck. Amazing Grace: 366 Inspiring Hymn Stories for Daily Devotions. Kregel Publications, Grand Rapids, Michigan, 1990.

John Maxwell. The Maxwell Leadership Bible. New King James version. Thomas Nelson Bibles, 2002.

The Congress of National Black Churches, Inc. (CNBC), The African American Devotional Bible (New International Version), Zondervan Publishing House, Grand Rapids, Michigan

Sid Buzzell, General Editor. The Leadership Bible (NIV): Leadership Principles From God's Word. Zondervan Publishing House: Grand Rapids, Michigan

Tokunbo Adelekan, African Wisdom: 101 Proverbs From The Motherland. Judson Press, Valley Forge, PA, 2004

Karkay Adrienne Tingba 10 Popular Liberian Adages and their Meanings. Koloqua Dialogues, Preserving the Liberian Story in Wetin Happen. May 2, 2019

Lulu V. Marshall, A Book of Liberian Parables: Wise Sayings and their Simple Interpretations. Archway Publishing, Bloomington: Indiana. 2015.

ABOUT THE AUTHOR

Samuel Broomfield Reeves, Jr., is pastor of the Historic Providence Baptist Church Monrovia, Liberia – West Africa – the Cornerstone of the Nation. Dr. Reeves is the former co-pastor of Madison Square Church in Grand Rapids, Michigan, USA. Dr. Reeves serves as an adjunct professor at the Liberia Baptist Theological Seminary in Paynesville, Liberia.

Dr. Reeves is the author of Congregation To Congregation Relationship: A Case Study of the Partnership Between a Liberian Church and a North American Church. He welcomes conversations with individuals, congregations, and mission agencies interested in this account of how cross-cultural partnership can transform the lives of people and faith communities into new understandings of mission in this globalized village. His other works include *The History of Providence Baptist Church: How Baptists Birthed, Led, and Influenced the Growth of Christianity in Liberia* and *Surveying the Leadership: Indispensable Qualities of Leadership*. His latest book, *Surveying the Leadership: Essential Characteristics of Leadership*, is a compelling sequel to *The Indispensable Qualities of Leadership*

BOOK REVIEWS

This sequel on ethical leadership is both compelling and challenging. The Rev. Dr. Samuel B. Reeves is a beacon of light to Liberia and the world in practice, preaching, and writing.

His Excellency, Joseph N. Boakai
President of the Republic of Liberia, West Africa.

"Here is a masterpiece about Biblically induced leadership's purpose, power, and philosophy. It radiates with the wisdom of the Master of Earth and Sea and Sky. Integrate these guiding principles into your life and become a diamond of a difference."

Dr. Isaac Newton,
*Political advisor, theologian, leadership consultant, development specialist, and co-author of the book: *Steps to Good Governance*.*

I am fully convinced that Rev. Dr. Samuel B. Reeves, Jr.'s profound leadership qualities are enduring, effective, positive, and universal. Practicing them will advance your family, community, religious institution, corporate Organization, and country. I highly recommend it to all aspiring and functioning leaders.

Hon. Linda Thomas Greenfield
Former United States of America Ambassador to Liberia
(2008-2012)

Relevant for all spheres of leadership, any place, and at all times, "Surveying The Leadership Landscape: Essential Characters of Leadership" blends the intelligence of integrity with the prosperity of peace. These sacred virtues are cloaked in mercy and justice, designed to advance the best outcomes when we influence others to transform the world for the better.

David Newton, MBA, MBBS, MD, Ph.D.
Vice President of the Greenville Medical Center in New Jersey.
He creatively combines public health, preaching, medicine, and
entrepreneurship to serve the underprivileged.

I have known Pastor Sam, as we called him at Madison, for many years. We joyfully served together as co-pastors at Madison Square CRC in Grand Rapids, Michigan. His book, Surveying the Leadership Landscape: Essential Characteristics of Leadership, is an excellent review of holistic and practical leadership. It encompasses planning, purpose, and achievement that contribute to good governance in the Church and the state.

Rev. David H. Beelen
Former Co-Pastor, Madison Square Christian Reformed Church
Professor, Calvin Theological Seminary, Grand Rapids, Michigan, USA

"Pastor Samuel Reeves transfers Nehemiah's leadership characteristics from the pulpit to public service. This book, above all, advocates that a sense of duty, diligence, dedication, and discernment pregnant with moral conviction is essential to any rebuilding project. I fully endorse these pragmatic insights. Apply them today."

The Rt. Hon. Dr. Denzil L. Douglas,
four-term Prime Minister of St. Kitts and Nevis (1995-2015) and current
Minister of Foreign Affairs, International Trade, Industry, Commerce and
Consumer Affairs, Economic Development, and Investment.

194

I would like to have the four-blurb highlighted above on the back of the book.

All things being equal, the African and African American Church faith communities, for the most part, follow the admonitions of their preacher. Two elements are operative here. First, African and African American communities are crisis communities by the very nature of the historic social pathology that exists, particularly in America. Therefore, the reality of the social order requires a response from the preacher. What does the preacher have to say about the state of crime, healthcare, mass incarceration, miseducation, and, yes, politics? Historically, people have turned to the preacher for moral leadership and divine direction. When the preacher speaks clearly and responsively on quality of life issues, the people will have a frame of reference steeped in trust and confidence in the man or woman of God.

Secondly, in most cases, the African and African American preacher is free to speak without permission from the oppressors and the established political order. This is the prophetic tradition of the African and African American preacher. The preacher's independence and freedom are directly linked to the power and precedence of biblical prophets. Prophets act and speak on behalf of the oppressed in the name of God. In short, they disturb the comfort and comfort of the disturbed. It is no coincidence that the towering leadership in the critical affairs of African and African American people has been concentrated in the preachers of the Social Gospel.

My friend and brother, Dr. Sam Reeves, stands in this rich prophetic tradition, providing consequential leadership in Liberia and beyond!

Rev. Dr. Christopher Allan Bullock
Senior Pastor,
Canaan Baptist Church
New Castle, Delaware, USA

Dr. Samuel Reeves is well-known as the Pastor of the historic Providence Baptist Church in Monrovia and President of the Liberian Baptist Convention. It has been my privilege to know and partner with Dr. Reeves. He has stayed in my home, preached at the Church that I pastor (First Baptist Church of Kings Mountain, North Carolina), and shared his vision for making disciples and growing congregations. He knows the characteristics needed for today's spiritual servant leaders. I commend to you the man and the book.

Rev. Dr. John (Chip) Sloane
Senior Pastor, First Baptist Church of Kings Mountain,
North Carolina

Surveying The Leadership Landscape: Essential Characteristics of Leadership* blends the intelligence of integrity with the prosperity of peace. It is an impressive model that influences others to transform the world for the better.

David Newton, MBA, MBBS, MD, Ph.D.
Vice President of the Greenville Medical Center in New Jersey.
He creatively combines public health, preaching, medicine, and
entrepreneurship to serve the underprivileged.

"Above all, this book advocates that duty, diligence, dedication, discernment, and moral conviction are essential to any rebuilding project. I fully endorse it for leadership impact."

The Rt. Hon. Dr. Denzil L. Douglas
4-term Prime Minister of St. Kitts and Nevis (1995-2015) and current
Minister of Foreign Affairs, International Trade, Industry, Commerce and
Consumer Affairs, Economic Development, and Investment.

Made in the USA
Columbia, SC
14 February 2025

53863550R00122